CALL IT THE LYRIC ESSAY

MW01137280

WE MIGHT AS WELL
CALL IT THE LYRIC ESSAY

WE MIGHT AS WELL
CALL IT THE LYRIC ESSAY

WE MIGHT AS WELL
CALL IT THE LYRIC ESSAY

WE MIGHT AS WELL

We Might As Well Call It The Lyric Essay:
A Special Issue of *Seneca Review*

Edited by John D'Agata and the graduate students of the Nonfiction Writing
Program at the University of Iowa

Seneca Review: Volume 44/2-45/1
Hobart and William Smith Colleges Press
Geneva, NY 14456

Copyright © 2014 Hobart and William Smith Colleges
ISBN 9781495123948 / ISSN 0037-2145

Printed by Canfield & Tack

Editor, *Seneca Review*: David Weiss

Design: Joshua Unikel

ESSAYISTS ON THE ESSAYS

ESSAYISTS ON THE ESSAYS

WHAT'S IN A NAME?

WHAT'S IN A NAME?

WHAT'S IN A NAME?

WHAT'S IN A NAME?

JOHN D'AGATA

It turns out there is an awful lot inside a name.

In 1903, in the February issue of *The Library World*, a leading journal on library management at that time, the head of a public library in Hampstead, England, published an article titled "The Fiction Nuisance and Its Abatement." William Doubleday was well-respected among his fellow librarians in England. He'd written a couple books on library science, as well as a decent work of criticism on Keats. So his article attracted some attention when it appeared.

"The Public Library is primarily educational in its work," Doubleday wrote. "Education is in the air, and with its efficiency is bound up the welfare of the nation."

At stake for Doubleday — besides the welfare of England — were the delicately impressionable minds of public library patrons, whom Doubleday noticed were starting to inquire about novels more than anything else at their libraries' information booths. Doubleday suggests that as many as 80 percent of patrons were now inquiring about fiction over other kinds of literature, adding that "we recognise that whilst some novels have positive value, others are at best harmless."

Hostility toward fiction was nothing new at the turn of the century. For hundreds of years throughout the English-speaking world, the growing popularity of fiction incited debates about the legitimacy of the genre: Would novels corrupt a nation's youth, did they deserve a place in libraries, were they even worth the paper they were printed on? Etc.

And on each of these questions Doubleday insists the answer is no. He does acknowledge that a library completely devoid of fiction would be shirking its duties as a cultural institution ("fancy a library without 'Don Quixote,' with no Scott, no Jane Austen, no Thackeray, no Dickens!"), but he nonetheless insists that the genre is not as serious or as important as others. Literature that is truly worthy of our time, he writes, "is a special form of literature read by young men." Why by young men? Because studious and serious young male readers "recognize the sternness of the battle of life," and they therefore "are resolutely preparing to face it" by applying themselves exclusively to "serious reading."

Doubleday never defines what he means by "serious" or "special" — nor why he thinks young men are its only admirers — but he nevertheless makes clear that fiction is not it. "The more elderly folk are, as a rule," he explains, "too hard-worked through the day to want to grapple with problems in their scanty hours of ease," which is why he places the fault for fiction's popularity squarely with those "leisured or semi-leisured people who not only confine themselves to works of fiction, but read them with astonishing haste and vigour. Materfamilias and her daughters, with some of the other sex, are to be found changing their novels three or four times a week with a zeal truly admirable were it employed in a better cause."

To help set the nation straight in terms of its reading tastes, Doubleday proposes that librarians start discouraging patrons from reading fiction by actively suggesting that they read something else:

> Selections of any books but novels may be produced upon request for the reader's choice . . .

or,

> In some libraries, borrowers have been allowed open access to all the bookshelves except those containing novels . . .

or,

> One common plan has been to allow borrowers to use a supplementary ticket, 'not available for works of fiction' . . .

and,

> Attractive works of non-fiction may be temptingly displayed in convenient showcases

— all of which Doubleday says he has tried at his own library, but with varying degrees of failure. "It is sad," he reports, "but not altogether surprising, to have to confess that most of the confirmed novel-readers are quite impervious to such allurements, and to reach them something more drastic will have to be tried."

Doubleday goes on to propose a bigger scheme in his article, but I'd rather not follow him down that hole. My interest in Doubleday lies in that final suggestion that he makes, which appears on page 207 in *The Library World*, volume V, issue 56, February 1903: "Attractive works of non-fiction may be temptingly displayed in convenient showcases." According to some linguists, this might be the very first use of the term "non-fiction" in the English language.

Now, before we lay a plaque here, it's worth noting that the *Oxford English Dictionary* suggests that the term "non-fiction" wasn't actually used until six years later in a different publication, *The Westminster Gazette*, in which a librarian reporting from a South African town claims to have succeeded in circulating a larger percentage of "non-fiction" and "more serious books — science, art, travel, biography, history, philosophy, essays, and the like — than novels."

But whichever publication wants to take the credit, it's clear that "non-fiction" emerged as a term among librarians in response to the perceived threat that fiction posed at the turn of the century in England.

Let me suggest that we forget the fact that Doubleday doesn't seem to have coined the term "non-fiction" in order to help him passionately explore the nooks and crannies of a peculiar new literary form, but rather so that he may dismissively refer with catchall efficiency to "everything that is not fiction."

And let's forget that every literary form that's included in that catchall — "science, art, travel, biography, history, philosophy, essays, and the like" — has its own origin story, as well as a complex aesthetic history that has developed over centuries, making it nearly impossible to reasonably conflate any one form in that list with anything else in the list.

And let's finally try to forget that if "fiction" comes from *fictio*, the Latin word for "make," then "non-fiction" essentially means "not art," precluding as it does the possibility of doing what art is supposed to do: *make*.

Instead, what bothers me most about the term "non-fiction" is that it emerged as a tool to defend provincialism — not to mention misogyny — and like most apophatic terms its purpose was entirely negative from the start, deployed by a didactic man with a small plot of turf he wanted to defend, interested less in celebrating what this genre actually is than in demarcating a border across which nothing else could pass.

Somehow, however, within the span of a single century, "non-fiction" has overshadowed half a dozen other literary terms to become the bland *de facto* banner that flaps above everything from journalism to memoir, imposing the same aesthetic standards and expectations on everything that falls beneath its shadow.

I am writing beneath its shadow now, in fact. As the director of the Nonfiction Writing Program at the University of Iowa, I grapple with the implications of the term on a daily basis. Whether it's dealing with inquiries from people who want me to proofread their cookbooks, or battling with university administrators so that my "non-fiction" students can receive the same "arts" fellowships as poetry and fiction students, by accepting the term "non-fiction" our community signals to the world that what goes on in this genre is at best utilitarian and at worst an utter mystery. I doubt any of us in the genre intended this to happen, but our adoption of "non-fiction" has done to our genre exactly what Doubleday had hoped it would: it has segregated us from art.

So a couple of years ago, when the editor of *Seneca Review* pointed out that I'd been editing the journal's lyric essays for about fifteen years, I asked if he'd give me his blessings to teach a yearlong course about *Seneca*, in which my class would explore how relevant lyric essays still are. From January 2013 through December 2013, my graduate students and I read and discussed every lyric essay that has appeared in *Seneca Review*, noting recurring trends, my embarrassing editorial ticks, and any peculiar aesthetic anomalies that emerged throughout the years, all in an effort to try to figure out what the lyric essay is, how it might be different from other sorts of "nonfiction," and whether there's still a place for such a thing in our culture.

And to help make our classroom conversations a little more consequential, I asked *Seneca* if it would allow the students to select their favorite fifteen essays from the journal, conduct interviews with the authors of all the selected texts, write their own critical essays to accompany each selection, and then package it all together in a special volume of *Seneca*. The result is now in your hands: a special issue of *Seneca* that is doubling as a book, and a book that has recorded our extraordinary year together.

A lot of students came to the course with suspicions about "lyric essays," and by the end of the year I think as many of them had become born-again believers as others had flipped over to skepticism. And that's the point. We ought to be questioning all of the ways that we talk about this art form — from the various names we give it, to the parameters that we think our texts ought to follow. We don't have a solid history of criticism in this genre. So what we think of it, and what we make of it, and what we know of it is up to us. If we want off the sidelines of literary history, we need to start producing our own criticism about the genre.

And then perhaps we ought to consider changing the genre's name.

ON THE PLEASURABLE PAIN
OF " THE PAIN SCALE "

ON THE PLEASURABLE PAIN
OF " THE PAIN SCALE "

ON THE PLEASURABLE PAIN
OF " THE PAIN SCALE "

ON THE PLEASURABLE PAIN
OF " THE PAIN SCALE "

HELEN RUBINSTEIN

INTERVIEW WITH EULA BISS
BY HELEN RUBINSTEIN

For a writer, an essay begins with an itch — an itch to know, to understand, to figure out. And an itch, as Eula Biss's father tells her in "The Pain Scale," is "just very mild pain."

The narrator of "The Pain Scale" is herself in some quite serious pain, pain that keeps her up at night and prevents her thoughts from reaching their conclusions. But her chronic and unresolved physical pain corresponds to an intellectual itch, one that begins mildly enough — with a doctor's request that she measure her pain "on a scale from zero to ten" — and becomes increasingly disturbing.

"A nasty itch," Biss writes, "can be much more excruciating than a paper cut, which is also mild pain. Digging at an itch until it bleeds and is transformed into pure pain can bring a kind of relief."

Biss's "itch" in "The Pain Scale" — the attempt, or essay, that drives her writing — is an effort to rank her pain on a scale bound by the ostensibly straightforward fixed points of "no pain" and "the worst pain imaginable." The attempt carries Biss into questions about the integers 0 through 10; concern about the aptness of quantification at all; and distress about the limits of imagination, mathematics, and memory. She uses the circles of Dante's *Inferno*, her conversations with her parents, and the Beaufort scale, which measures wind, to scratch at these problems. But scratching, as Biss has pointed out, does not nullify an itch. Instead, "digging at an itch" brings a *kind* of relief — the strange satisfaction of more itching and, eventually, a "pure pain."

Biss is concerned with the limitations of the pain scale's form, so it's fitting that she attempts to confine her own essay to a pain scale's zero-through-ten structure. The notion that an experience can be scaled down, so to speak, to the artificial limits of a pain scale is a provocation that invites readers into "The Pain Scale" from the very first glance, even if, as we read on, we don't know whether Biss's essay mocks the scale's structure, demonstrates its futility, or instead shows the scale's occasional usefulness. This flirtation between content and form is one of many uncertainties (or itches) that keep us reading on.

And as we read on, the essay unsettles us further: with provocations ("Is no pain desirable? Does the absence of pain equal the absence of everything?"); with curious contentions ("I am incapable of imagining the worst pain imaginable"); and with paradox, as Biss admits that she has come to find the "extraordinary pain" of treatment "deeply pleasurable," despite a medical definition of pain as necessarily "unpleasant."

If, for a writer, an essay begins with the itch of attempted understanding, then a reader turns to an essay with a desire to be unsettled, an itch that might be more mildly called curiosity. But as the writer scratches, as the questions and tensions of the essay intensify, the effort develops into a maybe-pleasurable pain that writer and reader share.

The writer's concerns become the reader's concerns, in other words; the writer's horrors, the reader's horrors. Biss introduces the horror of no evidence ("nothing to illustrate my pain except a number"); the horror of chronic pain's commonness ("Is this normal?"); the horror of math and medicine's unreliability ("the very use of numbers required a religious faith"); and the horror of not being believed ("It would not have occurred to me to think that I was imagining the pain"). The reader wonders, as the writer does, whether Biss will ever be able to tell her doctors if her pain is a 3 or a 4 or a 7 — and, finally, she cannot: she concludes that "the pain I am in is always the worst pain imaginable." This is not so much that Biss cannot imagine a level-10 pain, as she'd proposed at the start, but that her all-too-real current pain always obscures that theoretical "worst."

What Biss has landed on is a general human failure to relate, to communicate, and to empathize. The pain scale may seem like a tool for communication, but, as Biss's physician father has said, it exists partly to spare doctors their patients' pain: "Hearing someone describe their pain as a 10 is much easier than hearing them describe it as a hot poker driven through their eyeball into their brain." Biss's failure of imagination is not only a failure to place her own pain within some wider context of human pain, as she'd initially hoped she might, but also a failure to empathize with past and future selves. She cannot compare her pain to a painlessness she does not recall, or to a greater pain she might one day feel. She's dug at her itch, and it has bled. The "pure pain" of her devastating conclusion is indeed a "kind of relief."

As the pain scale is to Biss's physical pain, "The Pain Scale" is to her intellectual concerns — artificial, insufficient, limited by fixed points of beginning and end. Unlike the doctor's pain scale, however, Biss's essay succeeds at communicating with the reader the very real pain of a bothered mind. It's this success that marks the difference between the physical and the intellectual, the chronic and the temporary, what is lived and what is "only" imagined. Biss writes, "When I cry from it, I cry over the idea of it lasting forever, not over the pain itself." It's the lack of endpoint that makes her chronic pain so awful. And maybe it's the very limits of the essay form — the fixed points of first page and last, demarcating a space we can enter and exit at will — that make possible the shared empathy of "The Pain Scale."

Helen Rubinstein: Was the form of "The Pain Scale" integral to the essay's initial conception? How did it affect your thinking as you were writing?

Eula Biss: Yes. I rarely write form first — I usually find my form through the process of writing, which often involves some false starts. I initially began writing this essay as a more narrative, memory-based personal essay with conventional paragraphing. That form drew out some material that is still in the essay — some moments that involve my father — but it seemed to privilege the story of my personal experience with pain. This experience is what brought me to the essay, but writing about it directly was not offering me any new insights. I was frustrated with that first draft — I only wrote about two pages and then nearly a year passed before the idea of writing into the pain scale occurred to me. Once I began working in that form, the essay opened and began moving much more quickly. And this is usually how it goes for me — I don't know what form I'm going to write in, but once I find the right form I know it's right.

HR: Did working within this limited form affect your subsequent work?

EB: This essay served as a reminder of how form can facilitate content. I was not able to say what I wanted to say in this essay until I found the right shape for saying it. I always think of the film *The Five Obstructions* when I think of this — those formal elements that seem restrictive, or seem to be obstructions, are often what push the content where it needs to go. But there's another side to that, too. At some point I decided, in writing this essay, that I was going to write one page for each number on the pain scale. This caused me some trouble, as I had more to say around some of the numbers than others. Eventually I realized that there was no reason to write exactly one page for each number — this was an arbitrary limit rather than an essential formal element. Discerning between the two is often still tricky for me.

HR: In "The Pain Scale," your attempt to measure pain widens into an investigation of imagination, memory, measurement, wind, and numbers, but the essay never relinquishes its sense of control. Were there other inquiries, or lines of thinking, that you had to cut?

EB: To the extent that an essay tracks the movement of a mind, as Phillip Lopate would say, it is entirely a relic of process. I have a hard time separating process from product. In this case I was pursuing some questions around quantification and accumulating more questions along the way. The essay is composed of the bread crumbs that I dropped as I went. In the process of revision I swept many of those crumbs away. I cut anything that failed to open into further thinking, anything that felt too static or boring.

HR: Would you be willing to describe what you see as the difference between using a conventional paragraphing style (indentations without line breaks), and using the sort of line breaks you use in "The Pain Scale" and in some of your other work?

EB: Like a number of my essays, "The Pain Scale" is an associative essay — its logic is an associative logic. The relationship between the paragraphs in this sort of essay is like the relationship between stanzas in a poem. When paragraphs are acting like stanzas, I treat them like stanzas on the page.

HR: Your essay "Goodbye to All That" is closely modeled on Joan Didion's, and you've described copying Didion's essay word for word to "teach [your]self how to write." Previously, you'd trained as a painter, where copying masterworks was an essential part of an artist's education. Did you have any models in mind when you were writing "The Pain Scale?"

EB: I wasn't working from any particular model in this essay, but I was reading a lot of Anne Carson at the time. A friend of mine from college, Liz Werner, did a translation of Nicanor

Parra's "antipoems," titled *Antipoems: How to Look Better and Feel Great*, which got me interested in how functional forms like lists or recipes could be repurposed as literary forms. Liz did a public art installation of her own antipoems, and her work probably primed me to think of the pain scale in my doctor's office as a viable form for an essay.

A SPIRIT HOUSE

A SPIRIT HOUSE

A SPIRIT HOUSE

A SPIRIT HOUSE

LISA GRAY GIURATO

INTERVIEW WITH JENNY BOULLY
BY LISA GRAY GIURATO

In "Too Many Spirits Who Begged to Be Let In," Jenny Boully visits family in Korat, Thailand, where the boundaries between the world of the living and the ethereal spirits who permeate the landscape blur. Customs dictate that unless you provide an appealing home for the spirits, they will slip into your home, your place of business, and your nightly dreams, disrupting the orderly business of the living. Thais build spirit houses, small, intricately whittled wooden dwellings that, on first glance, can be mistaken for exquisite birdhouses. An owner will burn sweet incense, light candles, prepare food, and adorn the structure with garlands of flowers to entice the spirits of a place — wraiths in the trees, ghosts of monstrous tragedies in the mountains, ancestors living near the water, and loved ones who circle family homes. The spirit houses vary in their colors, which range from blue to red to brilliant gold, yet are always positioned in the same way, out of the shadows cast by the homes of the living.

Jenny Boully does the same with language. She wrote "Too Many Spirits Who Begged to Be Let In" to honor Deborah Tall, the editor of the *Seneca Review* for 25 years, who had recently passed away. To Boully, the essay is a literary form that creates space — a spirit house — to honor the dead so the living can keep writing. Her previous *Seneca* essay, "The Body," is a disembodied text, an empty page with only a title and footnotes. Its blankness supplants the subjective "I" of the traditional essay, forcing the reader to inhabit the essay's empty space. In "Spirits," she details the funeral practices of monks who tend to the dead and supervise the construction of spirit houses, writing, "At any ceremony, the monks will unravel a white string; it will keep going and going and going."

The string becomes the conduit through which good merit or good energy can be transferred from the living, whether in a funeral ritual or those setting up a spirit house, to the dead.

The string enables the living to free the dead from suffering through this transference of good merit; thus, freeing the living from ghostly hauntings from the unhappy dead. Boully weaves her own version of this white string throughout her essay, and as we read, we become part of the ritual. Imagine the lists of white things throughout the essay as the monks' string. Boully is herself a monk unwinding the white "funeral flowers," unfurling the white "crematorium smoke," the "rice," the "underside of the oyster mushrooms," and the "casket of the little girl." Boully tells us herself that she is following the ritualistic "need to, once more, catalog white things before reaching the conclusion to the essay."

Boully writes about ritual while at the same time she performs ritual through the refrains that are repeated. Imagine with each repetition of a word or a phrase, that Boully is circling back and unwinding more string with which to encircle us, to tie us into the ritual. "But she will be back; she will fly back and forth, back and forth: some things navigate space this way; the essay, for instance; love, for instance. But she will be back; she will fly back and forth, back and forth [...]." We are caught up on the winds of her circling refrains, following her trail of white string, caught up in the spirit ritual, the spi*ritual* performance of enticing the ghosts into a spirit house called the essay.

For ancient Greeks, poets were thought of as empty vessels through which the spirits spoke. With each exhaled string of words, an inspired lyric was constructed, creating the tenuous connection between the blurred spirit world and the living. The poet is the monk in a ritual, her words are the string, pulling us into the performance, encircling us as she channels all the spirits begging to be let into the spirit house she has written into existence.

Lisa Gray Giurato: It seems as if your essay navigates in multiple ways. We have the stories of your personal experiences in Korat, and there also seems to be a reflexive commentary. Do you see your "Too Many Spirits Begging to Be Let In" as a critical essay that is commenting on itself or on how essays in general function for you?

Jenny Boully: I very much see my essay as an essay on essays; that is, when writing it, I had in mind that this essay ought to comment in some way on not only the occasion of writing it (the passing of Deborah Tall) but also the mechanics of writing it. The task, as I understood it, was to write an essay on the lyric essay, but I also knew that the issue in which the essay would be included was in memory of Deborah Tall. So I had existence and being and the afterlife in the foreground of my writing. It seemed to me that the act of composition is so heavily intertwined with being and the need to emote, to let oneself be known, to exist, as it were, *in* the world.

LGG: So, as a critical essay, you are both commenting on the lyric essay as a form while at the same time embodying what the form of the lyric essay can provide for you, a space to write about our mortality?

JB: The lyric essay, whether one wants to acknowledge it as an essayistic subgenre or not, allowed me, at a time in my life when I most needed it, to write in a way that was intense and explorative. I was able to fill in the very corners of the page. I felt that I could explain away if I needed, retract, repose, return, restrain if need be. More than anything, it held the promise that writing could be exciting. There was a shiny newness about it, and I wanted to live in that flash.

LGG: You mention that you could return. It makes me think of how spirits circle houses and how you return back to certain refrains as well as ideas. There is a feeling of being immersed in a circling of arrangement on the page, like when you mention in the critical part of your essay how you wanted to "cut and paste" different sections.

JB: In composing the essay, I know that I simply delighted in the refrains, in the spin of meaning that a phrase could incur in a new context, how meaning could change by simply rearranging the paragraphs. For me, commenting on the form was also a way to comment on how sometimes, in living, we can't do as planned or the plan goes wrong or the plan changes or, worse, perhaps the plan never materializes at all — that what we hope and what we achieve are sometimes, painfully, two very different things.

LGG: Is this why you begin the essay with such a horrifying story? One that no one could ever imagine could happen?

JB: I think I began the essay with this story because it demonstrated just how quickly life could leave you, just how quickly a dear, precious, loved one could be taken from you.

LGG: That sense of loss, of hauntedness seems to be enacted in your return to these painful and unforeseen deaths. When someone dies, it's difficult to have a conversation about it and yet, there seems to be a human need to talk with others about painful events. Does the essay form give you a place to talk about loss?

JB: I return to it quite often in the attempt to unravel existence, my place in it, the overwhelming sense that the events keep pushing, temporally, further away from me. The moments in it I consider quite awesome, and I mean awesome in its strictest sense: these moments were full of awe, weighted with it, almost burdened by it. I wonder sometimes if I lived these moments at all, but the essay reminds me that I did and then I confront the knowledge of life and death and impermanence and oblivion again.

LGG: One last thing, if you could indulge me a bit more. I was watching *Animal Planet* with my kids, a reality TV show on how this guy builds dream tree houses and forts for people. A woman was describing to the builder how she wanted a tree house that was similar to a Thai spirit house. Forgive my ignorance on this, but I was not aware of the tradition of Thai spirit houses. I couldn't help but think of one of the images from your essay that still rattles around in my brain, of a boy's spirit circling a house begging to be let in. Is the Thai spirit house a part of the spiritual grappling with mortality that you are navigating in your essay?

JB: The Thai spirit house is quite a necessary thing. Unless you want to constantly be bothered with ghosts and spirits in the house where you live, you need to have one in your yard and bring gifts to keep the spirits happy with the little house lest they come to live in your house. If you've built a house, you've disturbed some spirits who will now need a place to live. Also, if someone in your house has died, they will surely want to come back and live where they have always lived. Therefore, the importance of the spirit house, so that all those who have lived on the land before you will have a place to go and not bother you and keep you up at night. The spirit house is an overarching symbol in the essay, but is itself just another symbol of how the living would much rather do just that: go on living.

THIS MASK IS NOT ENOUGH

THIS MASK IS NOT ENOUGH

THIS MASK IS NOT ENOUGH

THIS MASK IS NOT ENOUGH

QUINCE MOUNTAIN

INTERVIEW WITH ANNE CARSON
BY JOHN D'AGATA

Irony! Tony subverter of expectations. Tiny terrible sword in the fist of the weak. Here we have the master's tools razing the master's house; the reader knowing more than the characters; the aging not-quite-hipster with the T-shirt that says exactly what it does not mean: PORN STAR. Socrates found irony useful, responding to his accusers with trick questions and oblique, absurd truths. The poet Sappho did, too. For her, *irony* is a verb: something that one can use to distance oneself from one's life. Sometimes the surface doesn't match what's going on inside.

Anne Carson offers an essay on "my life" as Catherine Deneuve. Deneuve is an actor celebrated for her role as a lesbian Mrs. Robinson, a philosophy professor who's having an affair with a much younger female student. Carson dons a Deneuve mask. And underneath that mask, the Carson/Deneuve character boils with arousal and interest in her student; we sense an affair that could happen at any moment. Sappho is lying spread open on the floor, *deathless*, while Deneuve is lying on her bed, *dry from fantasy*. Often, in Carson's text, there's shame: *a rusty edge that Deneuve sits on*. We feel the precariousness of this edge. "Irony..." is red with it.

Our narrator does take reflective distance at times (*The victim in an ironic situation is typically innocent...*), but such remove, even when offered at its ironic best, does little to protect us viscerally from the story. Hence, its title — "Irony Is Not Enough" — and hence its juice.

Why, though, is it "not enough"? *Irony is no joke*, Schlegel warns. One problem, as Carson notes, is that in time, *one's mask / becomes / one's face*.

Once I was at dinner with a small group of artists and activists. A fiction writer had just given a reading — a short story about a jealous young woman who tore the stereo out of a boyfriend's car. Seated next to the writer was a man who makes his living as a performance artist, a street preacher amid consumers, railing against our democracy's every hypocrisy. The night of the reading, he clanged his spoon against a bottle of vegan salad dressing and asked that we all take a moment to consider the writer's courage in having told her story.

Eight or nine other nine other artists agreed. Clapping and finger snapping ensued. Even the climate change activist took his elbow out of the composer's mashed potatoes and agreed. So brave, he said. She says what everyone's afraid to.

Yes, she had shown us she was *that girl* — without apology. Everyone turned to the writer; it was her moment to accept the gratitude.

It's fiction, she said. Not memoir.

I thought her response withering, but no one withered.

Yes, yes — but very brave of you to share your story.

Even this sophisticated, literary, performance-savvy crowd could only approach the fiction writer's story as confession. Questions aside of how much a readership is ready to assume, especially when a woman is writing, that the character in question can only be the author herself. Questions aside of whether memoir is a form we now gender female, overall, and whether that form itself somehow becomes translated onto stories about women in general, especially when read aloud by female writers. I think it's safe to say that readers are all too ready to link characters and authors, especially authors who voice characters using first-person or close third-person narration.

That is my only explanation for Carson's next mask, the "Second Draft" version of this lyric essay. You'll find it in her collection *Men in the Off Hours*, a volume more widely known than the issue of *SR* in which the first version appears. In this second version, tercets are exchanged in favor of fourteen titled prose paragraphs, perhaps to ensconce us in a more familiar architecture of essay. We are told of the lecturer's desire for her student, but are seldom shown, and the allegory dries into a shallow muck. The deeper critical work suffers as well. We get fewer Sappho fragments and much less exposition on Socrates. We still see irony performed; even in revision, we are made to know that the streaming bits of fire and the professor's cool surface don't match. But Sappho's complex relational irony is exchanged for the cleaner, more straightforward irony that Socrates uses "to draw a veil over / the question that is jutting out from him. The veil [...] made of feints / and lesser proofs / and half-burnings."

Comparing Carson's later version (which she dubbed her

"2nd Draft") with the original version herein, you might ask yourself, as I did, why Carson would want to erase so much of her performance, why she would diminish her analysis so. Carson strikes me as nothing if not a brilliant and careful author. I don't think she'd bother to reword the selection for her collection if she simply didn't like it. I suspect rather an urgent dissatisfaction: a need not only to move on to other work, but to revise and republish what's been done, to wash away the old with the new.

I can't help but wonder if perhaps the problem is not with the essay itself, but with its readers. Maybe an audience all-too-interested in Carson's celebrated gift and mystique has simply proven itself incapable of meeting (or unwilling to meet) her allegory on its own terms. Perhaps the source of Carson-as-Deneuve's rusty-edged shame became a threat to real-life Carson, too. The setting is certainly close to home: a wintry campus, a graduate classics seminar... Maybe the mask fits too closely, and confuses.

In other words, maybe irony has its limits. Maybe it is "not enough" to protect Carson the poet/scholar, just as "It's fiction, not memoir" wasn't enough to protect the colony writer from the judgments of her conclusion-jumping cohort.

If I could ask Carson to reconsider her "2nd Draft" and stand by the version herein, I would. Apparently, those who did not like Solon, the Athenian coiner of coinage, liked to say of him: "He has a foreskin but for fear of wearing it out he uses another man's when he copulates." It's an early fiscal metaphor, one Carson quotes in her second version. The power of a good metaphor, according to Aristotle, springs from the truth beneath its mistakenness.

Before writing "Irony Is Not Enough" for Seneca Review, *Anne Carson sat down with John D'Agata for an interview on the banks of the Iowa River in Iowa City. This was her first-ever interview in the U.S.*

John D'Agata: I'm thinking about this really beautiful argument in *Eros the Bittersweet* about how you imagine Sappho and her peers being so close to the origins of their language. You say that it's no wonder so much of this early writing is love poetry, and no wonder so many of these love poems are so great. You say it's because there's perhaps no true lover suggested — no guy or gal that's literally intended in the poems — but instead that the real lover and recipient of this desire is language itself.

Anne Carson: Isn't that profound? See, you can have those kinds of ideas when you're young. So, yes, okay. That's good. I think I still believe that. Sappho is the best example, in my experience, of that original thing coming into the world. It's precious. It's like you had a world of people who couldn't see colors and that world was just a black-and-white TV to them. Then someone came into the world and clicked on color. It's that much different reading the words we have in English compared to those in Greek. They're turned around, the Greeks. Homer talks about how people are situated in time. He says they have their backs to the future, facing the past. If you have your face to the past, you just look at the stuff that's already there and take what you need. It's not the same as us, facing the future, where we have to think about that [points behind] then turn around and get it and bring it here, bring it in front of us. So I think for someone like Sappho it's not a question, it's just original. It's what's there. It's part of being.

JD: You told me earlier that you're more interested in an intriguing set of facts than you are in a story, and that what you create when you write is more of a nexus for the facts, some kind of narrative, some kind of anecdote or scenario to fit them into. Does your form then originate out of those facts that you discover and become fascinated with?

AC: I think it does. I think if we take facts to mean stuff in the world, like the way a lake is a fact, then yes.

JD: Is that what the form is trying to do?

AC: Yes, I think so. I think that that is a pure moment, when you see that a fact has a form, and you try to make that happen again in language. Form is a rough approximation of what the facts are doing. Their activity more than their surface appearance. I mean, when we say that form imitates reality or something like that, it sounds like an image. I'm saying it's more like a tempo being covered, like a movement within an event or a thing.

JD: Looking at most of your collected essays, just structurally or typographically, I see a lot of fragmented narratives. Especially those in *Plainwater*. Is that the effect of lots of facts at work?

AC: Facts are a substitute for story. Facts are useful to me because I don't have any stories in my head, so in the absence of story you can always talk about facts to fill the time. Right? I don't know what it has to do with fragmentation, though. What do you mean by a "fragment"?

JD: Well, I don't mean that the narrative is fragmented, I mean the essays, with all their sections, work like . . . collage, maybe.

AC: Oh, I see. Okay. Well that's a true insight, I've always thought of it as painting. Painting with thoughts and facts.

JD: Which is something that a straight narrative can't do?

AC: I would think not. Because in a straight narrative you'd have too many other words, too many other words that aren't just the facts. You're too busy trying to get from one fact to another by standard methods: *and; but; oh; no; then I was in this room; because; that's Patti*. These aren't facts; they're hard to paint.

JD: That's interesting. Because if your passion is coming out of Greek and the rootedness of Greek, fragmentation seems like it'd be closer to the thing than a straight narrative, which as you say imposes too much of Writer onto the facts.

AC: Right. The meaning is all padded, costumed in normalcy. I think probably my painting notion comes out of dealing with classical texts which are, like Sappho, in bits of papyrus with that enchanting white space around them, in which we can imagine all of the experience of antiquity floating but which we can't quite reach. I like that kind of surface.

LORD OF CONFUSION

LORD OF CONFUSION

LORD OF CONFUSION

LORD OF CONFUSION

BARRET BAUMGART

INTERVIEW WITH KATIE FORD
BY QUINCE MOUNTAIN

Two travelers pull over and stare at the multicolored strata woven through a crumbling rock face. They're on a road trip. We know nothing of their past. "We drove through Wyoming . . . in the mountains we saw no animals, no birds." We soon discover, however, that their future is uncertain. The two disagree about important things. The narrator sees mountains as a site where two forces converge and weave into one. Her partner sees mountains as "the foresight of division," a marker of separation, of two bodies slowly severing. Here, in the harmless speculations of two tourists, Ford unfolds a deeper and more lasting divide. Beneath the benign exchange about geology, we see a vast expanse separating two human beings.

Katie Ford's narrator would like to believe, after Donne, that there are no island universes, that each "is a piece of the continent, a part of the main." But her partner contradicts this desire. The words of D. H. Lawrence come to mind. All our troubles, he writes in *Classic Studies*, stem from the fact that "man insists on oneness . . . " when in reality " . . . each organism is isolate in itself." Fleeing this painful dichotomy, the narrator's mind plunges into the surrounding green hills where she ponders St. Catherine of Sienna who, "Desperate for communion . . . was beside herself in hills like these." We read in the narrator's frantic recounting of the ascetic's life a search for her own serenity. If true communion is impossible between people, might the narrator, like the envied saint exiled in the hills and starved into hallucination, achieve a mystical union with God? Catherine's only sustenance came from the communion wafer, "Downish hair covered her neck . . . she had constant stomach pain, but the records say nothing of doubt." Catherine experienced "One thing," that is, certainty. A lack of division. But the feeling didn't last. And neither did Catherine. "You have to kill a thing to know it satisfactorily," Lawrence wrote.

The narrator returns from the fantasy of oneness after

finding a crow's severed wing lying beneath a roadside marker that explains the ancient upheaval that built the mountains over Wyoming. "Lord of confusion," she declares, "Lord of great slaughter and thin birds, how could you answer both of us at once?" What the wing ultimately represents for the narrator, how exactly it allows her to continue on her journey, she does not say. But somehow the appearance of the fragile bird wing binds the narrator and her partner together. "There was nowhere to fix it. No talk of ever fixing it," she says as they drive on to Sheridan. It is the Lord of Confusion that this narrator worships: the confusion that led Catherine into the hills, the confusion that is the unproven theory of plate tectonics, the confusion that is an unknowable distance still isolating two minds. And placed before the backdrop of endless geologic time, Ford's essay refuses to resolve that division, as that would amount to a denial of life.

"Division" confronts the deep peril inherent in every human interaction. The essay does so in very few words — a single paragraph, a single page — achieving nevertheless a dizzying distillation. "God grant me the serenity to accept the things I cannot change, the courage to change the things I can, and the wisdom to know the difference." Our lives are defined by this tension, the oscillation between a desire to improve the world, but also not to destroy ourselves in futile projects. Throughout our lives we look for divining signs to recognize the difference, and, sometimes, we pray for guidance. Rarely do we stop to think that we do not know, nor that this uncertainty, more than anything else, makes life worth living. We make art in order to remind ourselves of this. Katie Ford's "Division" is an essay, and by that I mean an attempt to distill personal wisdom, to distinguish between that which is in our power to change and that which is not, something we must keep doing, whether we are writers or not, whether we accept the help of God or not.

Quince Mountain: "Division" is in our upcoming anthology of lyric essays. Did you submit it with that classification in mind?

Katie Ford: Since I was writing a book of poems at the time, I thought of "Division" as a prose poem, but [laughing] I don't mind it being called a lyric essay, either.

QM: Are you sure?

KF: The arguments over genre and classification don't entirely interest me, so no, it really doesn't bother me. The term "lyric essay," to me, makes an argument that the essay should be revivified with musicality and sentence rhythms that perhaps press the argument into a surprising manifestation. The need for the term shows a desire for music in the writer and reader, a desire that needs to be answered, I think.

There are forms I'm interested in that might have no classification, but I need them, really, quite desperately. As a writer, I'm asking, "What form will lead me? What will articulate this particular emotion or thought or doubt?" I feel desperate for the form to arrive that is apt or right. So my relationship to form is one of desperation, one of petition.

QM: How did that desperation play out as you wrote "Division"?

KF: I think the form reflects the pained voice of the speaker wanting to commune with what isn't communing. For me, the perfection on the page of the justified, locked print entails a kind of imposed communion, a pressure for the small narrative to articulate the pain of division. The braiding of the separate themes and images, for me, was a way to manifest the mind's simultaneous strands of thought, for better or for worse.

QM: What interested you about Catherine of Sienna?

KF: Catherine of Sienna decided, near the end of her life, not to eat anything except the Eucharist. She practiced what she considered a holy self-starvation, or inedia, and died of it in her very early thirties. She was constantly harming herself, but not for the sense of exhilaration of that harm. She did it so she would be able to stomach what she saw in the suffering of others, to toughen up, so to speak. She would eat the vomit of the people at the hospital as she tended them so that she'd be able to bear being with them. It seems she also, in her latter years, wanted her body to become entirely "made of" the host. It was a form of intimacy with Christ, as well as a way of replicating his suffering, and was one of the intimacies available to religious women at the time. She, for me, is an extreme example of being desperate for communion on all kinds of levels, and in "Division" the speaker is also battered with this desire, desperate for these two people to look at the land and think the same thing.

QM: When I read "Division," it was so clearly to me a theodicy essay. And even if it's not dealing with the problem of evil in its vilest incarnation, the theological stakes in these questions about separation, about beliefs on moving apart versus coming together, do strike me as vital here. Growing up evangelical, I was always taught that hell is eternal separation from God — that's it. Evil, then, was whatever causes the separation. In general, the idea that evil would overwhelm any of us is hardly surprising. But in "Division" we see how a rather daily human separation overwhelms. So if it's about theodicy, it starts with the smallest, banalest crack. And even if there's any hope in the speaker's idea that the land is creased together, not separating, there's still a rift in the perceptions of the players involved. So I hooked into a tone of resignation and supposed that as your response to the gulf between person and person, maybe even between God and person.

KF: I agree separation is a kind of hell. I wouldn't use the language of "evil" for "Division," although maybe that's how it rings out for others, which is just fine, of course. My brain is ruled by things that are problematic theologically, whether I like it or not. The question of the distance or near proximity of God is, as far as I can tell, not something a human has knowledge about, yet I do think we have knowledge of the distances between us as humans.

The overt theological question in "Division" is this: *Lord of Confusion, Lord of Great Slaughter and thin birds, how could you answer both of us at once?* Our desires conflict. One person who prays for rain and another person who prays for sun in the same region cannot both be answered in a positive way, to put it simply. But the piece ends with the rather slight human assault in the night — someone keys the car of the couple as they sleep in a hotel in Sheridan. Sheridan, it's a small town, the couple is en route somewhere, and the deepest division is the slightest thing, this assumption: this will never be fixed.

QM: The best the speaker can do, amid these rifts and scratches, is to move on. Is that resolution, or simply resignation? Or maybe it's both. Divinity school — was that good for you?

KF: [Laughing] Was it a good idea?

QM: You went from Iowa to there? I mean, why not religious studies, or something else?

KF: I first went to Divinity School, then to Iowa. I went to Harvard to study theology, and yes, world religions, ancient language, and so on. It was really an intuitive decision. I wanted to study, I wanted to read — I mean in the old-fashioned way of "go read your subject; go read your problem." So before I went to the University of Iowa, I went to divinity school, and I read my problem as deeply as I could.

THE THREATENING THING

THE THREATENING THING

THE THREATENING THING

THE THREATENING THING

G. V. DE CHOISY

INTERVIEW WITH MICHAEL IVES
BY G. V. DE CHOISY

The threatening thing about turds is that they speak to the spirit's dependence on a temporary vessel of flesh. He who shits, eats — that thing gods never have to do. And in *The Dark Burthen* — an essay in the form of a diary, about shit — we find a narrator who is deeply preoccupied with his mortality, which is to say: with legacy.

The diarist's notations are obsessive. His observations bode threateningly: "Nov 8 Mottled and woundy this morning, like the fur of a vanquished hyena." Quickly, introspection emerges (doesn't it always?) alongside scatological description: "The anus as articulator, and excrement the speech of physical ailment." Feces are sure evidence of the body's inevitable demise. The diarist knows this; he has a body, he is a body, and so his record darkly goes, both fascinating and repulsive...

...And totally hilarious. *Vanquished hyena*? Come on. Who writes about poop this way? More to the point, who keeps a diary with language like this? Psychoanalytic theory says anal function and the symbolic transcendence of mortality often get confused in children; hence, the playground poop joke's omnipresence. As dark as the diarist's *Burthen* is, most of author Michael Ives's entries — "June 10 (Underwater Ziggurat)," for example — are uproarious. Is that to say the project and its approach are childish? Actually, yes, a little. Thank God. It must be so. It takes a particular perspective — one borderline naive, if not outright infantile — and some kind of resilient whimsy, some magical tendency toward silver linings, to examine the evidence of one's own decay, and not draw dire conclusions.

Ives begins *Burthen* with an epigraph from Ecclesiastes (1:8): "The eye is not satisfied with seeing." What we see, we translate, in other words. We can't help but make meaning of our surroundings and circumstance. Whether the meaning we make is positive or negative is another matter entirely. For three days, the diarist's view goes bleak:

Oct 16 I see nothing, nothing more than filth.
Oct 17 I see filth.
Oct 18 Again, filth.

— a rough outlook, to say the least. But the diarist rallies after his three-day slump — "Oct 20 Okay, a lambda ... " — and returns to his toilet seat philosophizing: "Time is an invisible worm: its peristalsis is the days, and months and years; its feces physical manifestation." But what's the thing going wrong inside? Is it cancer? Is it Crohns? If Ives hears a diagnosis, we don't. We're left to speculate about his health. To do so for long would be entirely beside the point. If the diarist's fears are correct, this epistemological journey isn't going to end with a neat revelation. It's going to end with his death. There's no time for the navel-gazing style of introspection endemic to conventional illness narratives. If we're going to get to the bottom of things, well then, to the bottom of things we go. Ives has to drop his gaze down to his exploding, foreboding sphincter. If it is childish, this approach, then so be it. *Memento mori*, you know? If we can't laugh about the end, we're as good as there already.

The first time I read *The Dark Burthen*, I thought about my father. He says all he wants on his gravestone is an exclamation point on one side and a question mark on the other. It's up to him, of course, but I'm not convinced. He's a potter, my dad — a porcelain ceramicist of no small renown. It would be fitting, I tell him, if he threw his own urn. "Your opus and your omega," I tell him in his studio. In the hospital I tell him jokes. He spends more time there, lately.

I haven't shared *The Dark Burthen* with Dad. Instead, I've been reading and rereading it for my own sake. *Burthen* is pocked with hints of illness, but the illness is a metaphor. It's likely that Michael Ives hasn't undergone the poisonous violations of chemotherapy. It's likely he's never had a colostomy bag tear in the cereal aisle of a grocery store. No abscess has burst inside his gut, in the middle of a transatlantic flight, on route to his daughter's high school graduation. Ives's essay is still about what it means to be alive, and stuck on a trajectory toward life's inescapable end. Would that there was a pill to help us figure out that arc. There's only language. There's only the meaning we imbue language with.

Something odd happens to *Burthen*'s chronology toward its end. The diary entries stop in December, but Ives backtracks right after November 6, retreating to November 4 and then proceeding, for a second time, to November 5. This could be a slight of editorial hand — we're told this essay is an excerpt, after all — but I don't think that's it. Earlier in the essay, Ives writes: "Shit interrupts the dissociative dream, even if the interruption is itself only another layer of dream. Shit may be the closest equivalent to the *nunc stans*."

Nunc stans is Latin for "abiding now," the notion that time isn't actually marching us forward, that there is no trajectory of past flowing into a present capable of extending itself into some promise of a future. But *The Dark Burthen* rejects shit's timeless equivalent. By engaging his topic in the form of a diary, Ives transfigures his feces into "sculpted hyphens between what I've been and what I am," turdly ellipses resisting stasis, struggling toward some semblance of progress. By messing with the diary's expected linear form, Ives affords himself a tremendous freedom, enviable, and almost godlike: he has rendered his days such that he can return to them, whenever and in any order he wishes. He has a made a medium of his time and its contents, shaped and colored with language that is smarter, funnier, and more intimate, perhaps, than thoughts on death and shit have any right to be.

It's easy enough to say a piece of writing belongs to one genre or another, and easier still to say why the bad stuff is bad. Remember October 16? "I see nothing, nothing more than filth." Go stick your foot in the ocean sometime. I bet you'll brush up against something fecal. A work of art is shitty because shit abounds, it's on everything, in everything. Good art is good because it comes from mere mortals who, having seen this abundance, are unsatisfied. They bear witness by trying to see something more and then, if the filth isn't beyond seeing, they make something different and better from it. Not shit, but "a lambda (lowercase), the pediment of a bungalow . . ." Not shit, but "swollen rolls of cinnamon bark this morning, as of a raft disassembled by cruel seas."

At one point, Ives invokes Georges Perec — "What can we know of the world?" — and answers in concert: "I reiterate what the true ascetic realizes: if you want to know the world, circumnavigate your own ejecta." Here is a lesson worth recording. If you want to know what you're about, don't stray so far, and don't look "inside yourself." Just look at what you've made.

G.V. de Choisy: *The Dark Burthen* appropriates a diary's form, ostensibly, for a diagnostic record. How much of that *isn't* allegorical?

Michael Ives: *Burthen* arose out of a rather intractable case of creative constipation several summers ago. In a fit of rage, worried that the summer was draining away and I was getting nowhere, I described a fictitious, if plausible, "deposition." Like a four-year-old getting back at his parents. The idea of a journal became clear to me, and I ran with it, as a daily exercise: to describe my own feces as if I were an entomologist describing a new species of wasp, or Ruskin in some architectural ekphrastic throes.

GVC: But you stuck with shit?

MI: Through the act of writing the thing, I actually performed a kind of diagnostic meditation on something I truly abhorred. I am not given, in the least, to toilet humor, or scatalogico-verbal play; it makes me quite uneasy, in fact. I was contending, as I wrote, with all sorts of unexamined prohibitions.

GVC: Why feces, though, as opposed to blindness, or a loss of speech?

MI: I came to writing after a deep immersion in music; specifically, jazz. I'm always looking for something like a "key," some precalibrated way into the thicket of experience. At the same time, unhappily, I'm rather suspicious of "hooks" — guiding metaphors, any sort of "vehicle" that, however efficacious, threatens to overmaster my sensitivity, my fidelity, to the articulation of any particular experience. A Bateson-ian double bind. And shit was just the thing to undo that bind.

I became interested in the idea of confronting resistances of all sorts. This topic seemed a perfect vehicle for exploring them. The "author" (who "is" and "is not" me) had no choice but to overdescribe what he saw as a form of belle-lettristic defense. The writing is florid, absurdly so — it means to celebrate the wildly inventive potential of sublimation, at the same time that it "thinks" it's confronting sublimation. Some of the descriptions are more like Rorschach projections than objective delineation. But that's part of the comedy.

GVC: The best comedy retains an edge (or more) of tragedy, of reality. What would you say to someone who read *Burthen* literally?

MI: I never underestimate the imperial reach of literalism, but I think you're driving at something far more interesting. There's one moment where the narrator worries that he wouldn't be able to see blood in his stool because of his color blindness. Other than that, there's no obvious mention of serious gastrointestinal distress in the entire piece. What, though, might that very silence mean in the face of what could be a dire case of colitis, or the like? One would have to assume that his obliviousness to his own physical viability represented something like a linguistic redemption. Though, really, that would amount to arranging subordinate clauses on a digestive Titanic.

GVC: But you're comfortable with fictitious elements in essays, plausible or otherwise. Many aren't.

MI: The fiction/essay blur is complicated, and I suspect, largely an issue of context sensitivity. Certain occasions seem to demand fidelity to what we call "real life." Then again, the true crime genre has been shaken repeatedly by instances of creative . . . "elaboration." What's interesting to me, at a meta-categorical level, is this very instability. It might reflect fluctuating attitudes toward what we think of as matters of fact, or givenness, and imaginative prerogative. *Burthen* is a total interpenetration of fiction and essay. In our time, perhaps because of marketing imperatives, the demands of expediency, experiments like this are apt to be filed under the heading of "lyric essay."

GVC: And you're content with that category?

MI: Honestly, I don't know. I'll leave such designations to others. I suppose the surface textures of *Burthen*'s language might be characterized as "lyric." That's being stupidly literal, though. Thomas Browne's *Urne-Burial* is, to my ear, as lyrical as English prose can get, and yet . . . well, perhaps it was among the first "lyric essays."

GVC: Couldn't "lyricism" also connote a tacit exchange between writer and reader? One where the latter is asked to work to supply meaning?

MI: You're absolutely right. I think I may be even more interested in the contract between world and writer. To fulfill those terms, we're somehow encouraging a spacious movement of responsive minds, as if accompanied by the Apollonian instrument of "musical apprehension." So we get "lyricism" from "lyre," right? And that wonderful homophonic surplus, "liar," in the bargain.

WATCHING WAYNE

WATCHING WAYNE

WATCHING WAYNE

WATCHING WAYNE

WATCHING WAYNE

LAWRENCE YPIL

INTERVIEW WITH
WAYNE KOESTENBAUM
BY LAWRENCE YPIL

It is not surprising that in "The Task of the Translator," Koestenbaum takes on the Benjaminian question by telling the story of a ménage à trois. Daisy, a poet, writes poems which are translated by Gavin and taught by Wayne. It is a simple enough premise: writer, translator, and teacher-critic, triumvirate of the translation triangle. Although in Koestenbaum's hands, this configuration is as much critical and academic as it is fundamentally erotic. Daisy and Gavin have an affair while Wayne watches. Daisy and Gavin break up, get back together, while Wayne teaches. Wayne takes Daisy out for a drink. Daisy decides to stop seeing Gavin. Gavin hooks up with Wayne. As in a game of musical chairs, Daisy, Gavin, and Wayne switch places. As in a dance of anything-goes, each one takes turns in each other's arms, each one reaching into each other's pants. As in the loving, so in the writing. Daisy's originals are at first translated by Gavin and taught by Wayne. But then at some point, Gavin begins to write his originals, which Daisy translates. We quickly find out that things end up disastrously, so everyone returns to their original positions.

By avoiding the conventional discourse of exposition and explanation and opting for narrative and allegory, Koestenbaum is able to not just investigate the concerns of translation, but also enact its very questions. In the process of moving from an original work to its translation to its eventual reception by a reader, who deserves the credit for its success? When much of the work of translation depends on a kind of mediation between languages and forms, how are we to regard the fate of the original text? What is the task of the translator?

It is a difficult question, the last one, which appears to be the heart of Koestenbaum's essay, being its title. It becomes especially difficult when we realize through this story of a threesome, that the process of translation is enacted not just through Gavin, the designated translator of this ménage à trois, but also in Daisy and Wayne. Writing, we realize through Daisy, becomes an attempt to translate her pain and breakdown into words. Wayne, likewise, in his attempt to understand the work of both Daisy and Gavin, is also merely trying to translate his fascination with the subject to his class, and to himself. The burden (and pleasures) of translation is shared by everyone.

By choosing to depict this process through a relationship of three, Koestenbaum liberates translation from the mere psychology of one. The question of translation is therefore taken from the realm of aesthetics to that of social relationships: dynamic, collaborative, and most important for Koestenbaum and for us readers — erotic. It is driven by desire, rather than fidelity. It is permeated by lack and frustration rather than fulfillment and stability. It borders on the absurd. At some point in the story, Gavin begins to translate a text that Daisy has not finished writing yet. Gavin is worried that Daisy is not composing quickly enough. Wayne is worried that Gavin is not translating quickly enough either. Koestenbaum enacts through the fluidity of their relationships the very slipperiness of language itself, the slipperiness *between* languages. If there is anything that embodies this tentativeness of meaning, it is the translated text: blatant in its status as being one of many possible versions of an original, and both frustrating and pleasurable precisely for the same reasons. When we deem a translation successful, we do it knowing that we are probably missing something from the original. We also know that there might be better translations in the future. But for the moment, if we are not happy, then we are at the very least tentatively content.

Ultimately, what's exposed in "The Task of the Translator" are the very reasons we continue to regard translation as if there is something about our lives that is wonderfully captured by this process. "Wayne" in the essay, is the true hero of the story: he who watches and waits and teaches and videotapes and fantasizes and obsesses. When Gavin, toward the end of the essay, kills himself in front of a crowd after receiving an award (a kind of death, so to speak, not of the author but of the translator), Daisy rushes to the stage to embrace his body. Wayne keeps a copy of the acceptance speech. Koestenbaum delivered this essay in an academic panel on translation, and I can't help but think of this essay as a critique on the contemporary interest in translation: its obsessions and fantasies, its fetishes (both exhibitionistic and voyeuristic) and longings.

Is "The Task of the Translator" an essay on desire in the

guise of a treatise on translation? Or is it an essay on translation in the guise of a story of desire? We are thankfully, pleasurably, back in the Koestenbaum bind of one or the other. "Wayne" would say, without a doubt, "all of the above."

Lawrence Ypil: In "the Task of the Translator," I got the sense that you were attempting to capture the complexity, the difficulty, and also the mischief involved in the process of translation. I also felt you were making some kind of commentary on war. What were the circumstances surrounding the writing of this essay?

Wayne Koestenbaum: Yes, mischief. Translation involves traducing, trespassing, betraying; benign theft; illicit ventriloquism; inevitable error. And yes, war. I wrote the essay in a time of war, of mobilization toward war. Perpetual war. For me to think about translation, and about Walter Benjamin, I needed also to remember and to be awake to present-tense war, to "foreign relations," "foreign affairs." The very notion of "foreign" as foreign. I wrote the essay (which I consider also a "short story" or a work of fiction) as my contribution to an academic panel on the nature of translation. I remember thinking that I was unfit to say anything responsible about translation, and that the only accurate statements I could make must travel through the canal of a fictionalizing voice. At the time, too, I was deep into the writing of a couple of novels, including Moira Orfei in Aigues-Mortes, and a fictional voice most snugly suited my capacities.

LY: So "Wayne" in the "The Task of the Translator" is a fictional you?

WK: Wayne in "The Task of the Translator" is sometimes me and sometimes not. I'm always present in everything I write, whether or not I use the first-person pronoun. But the selves I describe in my writing — even in my most seemingly transparent autobiographical writing — dwell a discrete distance from who I "actually" am. The instant I put myself into a sentence I start behaving falsely toward the actual. Certainly the tone of these sentences I'm now writing, though they use the first-person pronoun and are trying to be truthful and sincere, is accidentally deviating — a marked deviation — from the "real" circumstances, whatever they may be.

LY: In addition to novels, you also write poems. What role has poetry played in your essays?

WK: Everything I write in prose is informed by my life and experience as *poet*. To write a sentence, or a phrase, I must first listen to the silence preceding the words. Out of that silence (sometimes almost instantaneously) a cluster of words arrives, in a specific rhythm, with specific sonic properties and tics and idiosyncrasies. I am more aware of the process of listening than I am aware of the process of thinking. Thinking, for me, is a subset of listening. And listening — is that the property of poetry? Maybe not exclusively. But being a poet has solidified my orientation toward a listening that precedes and subsumes thought.

LY: In "The Task of the Translator" you use the segmented form. What draws you to this form?

WK: Segmented: a nice word. Like an insect's body. Gregor Samsa's. The freakishness and "foreignness" of the segmented body. I adopted the form many years ago. It came to me originally through such writers as Leonard Michaels and Donald Barthelme, long long ago, when I was primarily a fiction writer. And then, when I defected from fiction into essay, I found in the works of Sontag and Barthes and Michel Leiris (L'âge d'homme) and Ponge (Le savon) and Walter Benjamin a justification for fragmentation-as-method. My adoption of seriality as opposed to sequentiality (if there's a strict difference between them) permits me to build an essay from monads, and to cluster and stack the modules with an abstract temperament, aiming for covert resemblances and correspondences, subterranean affinities between paragraphs that aren't paragraphs and aren't stanzas but are boxy containers for sentences, sometimes very small boxes and sometimes large.

LY: I always feel like you are looking at things askance, using the essayist's prerogative of speaking about one thing by speaking about something else: translation, for example, and the slipperiness of erotic relationships — or the other way around. It reminds me of flirtation and innuendo, of deflection and gossip.

WK: Yes to deflection, dispersion; yes to the askance, the peripheral, the oblique, and off-topic. I've explored this issue and attempted to justify it more programmatically in my essay on Roland Barthes, "In Defense of Nuance," which appears in *My 1980s & Other Essays*. I turn to Roland Barthes as supreme exemplar and defender of the philosophy of swerving, of deflection. He calls it the realm of the "obtuse" meaning. I take Barthes's obtuseness and give it a more comic and prurient turn. I swerve not in pursuit of the neutral but in obedience to the giggle. Part of the listening process, described above, is listening to the wrong turn the imagination is taking, the turn toward the filthy and the obscene and the trivial and the nonsensical. I listen not for the arrival of lofty sentiments — for sublimity — but for pratfall and flash (as in "flasher") and burp.

1001 CONTEMPORARY BALLETS:
AN AUDIENCE PERFORMANCE

1001 CONTEMPORARY BALLETS:
AN AUDIENCE PERFORMANCE

1001 CONTEMPORARY BALLETS:
AN AUDIENCE PERFORMANCE

HELEN RUBINSTEIN

INTERVIEW WITH
RICHARD KOSTELANETZ
BY HELEN RUBINSTEIN

Richard Kostelanetz's excerpt from *1001 Contemporary Ballets* opens with an epigraph by Lincoln Kirstein about a "good libretto," a "perfect type plot," a "dramatic narrative," and the "story of the Prodigal Son." The essay begins, in other words, with the question of story.

And it's an essay made up of twenty-five tiny, discrete stories — potential ballets, sketched in miniature. These start with scenarios we quite easily imagine: "Two impresarios try to steal each other's dancers, in full view of each other"; "a young man...falls in love with her and she with him." But the ballets soon poke fun at our assumptions about narrative. They have too much action, or none at all ("On the white classic leotards of scores of dancers are projected both radical contemporary political slogans and abstract lines"); they have wild dramatic arcs, or they flatline ("the prima donna was also a skilled automotive mechanic"); the performers become the audience, or vice versa (the audience's "commotion becomes the ballet"). Taken in chorus, these ballets demand, What is a complete story? What is a beginning or end? What "counts" as action? These are the questions that make *1001 Contemporary Ballets* an essay.

It's an essay performed by the reader, however, more than it is enacted on the page. It's the reader who will be tempted, for instance, to read the list of ballets as a refutation of the epigraph's assertion that "the perfect type plot for a dramatic narrative ballet [is] the story of the Prodigal Son." It's the reader who will be tempted to read the very last of the ballets presented here — "Christ is reborn in an urban slum, experiencing again, after a period of miraculous good deeds, a crucifixion and resurrection" — as somehow in conversation with the epigraph: a capitulation to its truthfulness, or a mockery of its suggestion that there could be some "perfect type plot" at all.

How we read this last ballet, though, depends on what has come before, and this is where a critical reading of Kostelanetz's essay — an attempt at discerning some static meaning in all its imaginative commotion — becomes thorny. Because the ballets' positions are fixed on the page, they appear to have been arranged in a certain order, and the reader will search for pattern in their sequence: Do the ballets change, as they go on? Do they increasingly challenge our expectations? Do or don't these ballets "develop"? These questions are another way of asking, What kind of story does this list of ballets tell?

The resourceful reader will learn, however, that in fact Kostelanetz has not arranged the order of these ballets at all. Instead, he's left their selection and arrangement to the editors of the various publications in which these excerpts have appeared. This gesture — the transfer of responsibility, or authority, to an outside editor — prefigures the transfer of authority to the reader that happens in any reading of *1001 Contemporary Ballets*. It's the reader who must attempt to make sense of the ballets before her, the reader who must essay. It's in your hands, says Kostelanetz, as he has with so many of his projects: his "counter-authoritarian publishing experiment," *Assembling*; his anti-authoritative *Autobiographies*, a self-portrait from multiple perspectives. Make of us what you will, these projects say, or what you must.

Even the *Ballets*' epigraph evidences a kind of handing-off, a relinquishing of power on the part of its author. The claim about "the perfect type plot for a dramatic narrative ballet" comes not from Kirstein, writer and cofounder of the New York City Ballet company, but from his NYCB cofounder Georges Balanchine: "Balanchine once said the perfect type plot was ...." Moreover, the claim is a thing "once said" — not stood behind over time, but tossed off casually, perhaps even in jest.

Balanchine-via-Kirstein's claim is as speculative, and as inconclusive, as Kostelanetz's essay itself: the ballets are sketches, mere propositions; even their order is malleable, unfixed. Because the *1001 Contemporary Ballets* has never been published as a whole, too, the entire work is — like each of the ballets it collects — more hypothetical than actual. It's as though the best glimpse we might get of the 1001 were sidelong, as though we cannot look at these 1001 head-on. Intentional or not, the very fragmentariness of Kostelanetz's project suggests an argument about the impossibility of seeing any "whole story."

Which might be as far as the reader can go, with the question of what sort of story this collection of ballets tells. It's a story about storytelling, certainly. A story-resistant story, a fragmentary story, an incomplete story. Exactly the sort of story we might call an essay — because if there is never any "whole story," then the story that resists storytelling is the story that seeks truth.

Helen Rubinstein: How did *1001 Contemporary Ballets* come about?

Richard Kostelanetz: I wanted to write texts that would suggest physical movements, even if they weren't realized, much as some Conceptual Art suggests aesthetic experience through words alone.

HR: Do you have any exemplary works in mind?

RK: In my mailbox in Southern Queens last month I found *The Bible 2.0* by Nathan Smithe, whom I think once shook my hand. As an extrapolation from the sacred text, which is a move I've made myself, it struck me as thorough, witty, and, yes, aesthetically profound.

HR: The Kirstein epigraph accompanies your other excerpts from this work as well. Could you discuss its significance, or the significance of his *Ballet Alphabet*, to this project?

RK: I like to quote Kirstein, in part because a teacher important to him at Harvard in the mid-1920s, S. Foster Damon, was later most important to me at Brown University around 1960. Don't forget that Kirstein was also among the first serious dance critics in America, though, given his other activities, that achievement is often slighted.

HR: You've sometimes suggested that ballets excerpted from *1001 Contemporary Ballets* be published in any order, as per an editor's selection. What defined the boundaries of this particular excerpt?

RK: As each "ballet" is a discrete text — without ostensible connection to any other — they can appear in any order. To the entire text there is neither beginning nor end. Not all from the original manuscript need be used. As readers are *not* supposed to connect the ballets, as they are meant to read and appreciated one at a time, I've encouraged editors to put as much vertical space as possible among them.

For over three decades now, I've liked to offer periodical publishers the opportunity to select and order to their tastes under the general principle that: Me write, you edit. And publish.

Most of my publishers, given such an opportunity, realize what I couldn't, to their credit and with my gratitude.

HR: Do you consider the *1001 Ballets* an "essay," "poem," "fiction," "lyric essay," or something else?

RK: Scenarios or scripts; more specifically, conceptual dance.

HR: Did you in fact compose 1001 of these?

RK: Probably not that many. I think the most recent manuscript had the number 201.

HR: I find *Contemporary Ballets* tremendously fun to read, partly for its unrelenting surprise, and partly for the pleasure of imagining these performances. It makes me wonder what the writing process was like: as much fun?

RK: May I claim to wanting to be the most surprising author ever — not just variously surprising but profoundly surprising — or at least in American literature?

Hearing about readers surprised by my work no longer surprises me.

HR: I can imagine that if surprise is your modus operandi, then it would become unsurprising. In order for surprise to continue, it seems it would need to be deliberately modulated or modified. How do you manage that?

RK: Huh?

HR: If "surprise" were always the driving force behind your work, I can imagine that in fact becoming flat, or dull. Actual surprise seems to rely on change — a shift from the expected — but if you expect surprise, then surprise is not surprising.

RK: *Huh?*

HR: Did you surprise yourself in the writing of these ballets?

RK: Sure, simply because I'm continually broaching territories I've not entered before. I tend to work with generative constraints that, once defined, surprise me with a wealth of options.

HR: Is there anything else you'd like to tell us?

RK: Richard Kostelanetz is the taken name of a kibbutz/commune composed of fifty industrious elves, none of whom competes with any of the others, all of whom physically resemble each other, each known to the others only by the Roman numeral visible on both the front and back of his T-shirt. III drafts performance scripts, aka plays and ballets, that aren't often produced. V experiments with alternative expositions such as this elves' inventory. XXI practices radical autohistoriography, representing his life and activities in a variety of alternative ways. XXX is the oldest guy bodysurfing in the NYC Rockaways. XLIII is their shrink- and mother-in-residence whom the others regard as a goof-off. XLVII, charged with curating their collection of more than 30 running feet of long-playing records, hundreds of tapes in several formats, and more than 20,000 books, is rarely able to find anything. XLIX tries in vain to keep track of the others, pretending to be the captain of a team that does not follow him. L, commonly called "El Elf" or "Elf El," ostensibly responsible for publicizing their activities, has conned the world, apparently successfully, into regarding RK as a single human entity.

VERSUS THE MIND AND
THE HARVARD OUTLINE "

ON " OUTLINE TOWARDS
A THEORY OF THE MINE
VERSUS THE MIND AND
THE HARVARD OUTLINE "

ON " OUTLINE TOWARDS
A THEORY OF THE MINE
VERSUS THE MIND AND
THE HARVARD OUTLINE "

JOSHUA WHEELER

INTERVIEW WITH ANDER MONSON
BY JOSHUA WHEELER

An outline is a plan for an essay to come or an essay unfinished or an essay not yet begun. An outline is skeletal on the page — "scaffolding so white against the language." An outline is all the bones of an essay without any of the flesh.

And yet, this one breathes.

See the spine, unsettled in the title, *Outline Towards a Theory of the Mine Versus the Mind and the Harvard Outline.* These topics will be our backbone, the vertebrae that don't quite fit together, that scrape and grind as the essay comes to life. Why is the mine at odds with the mind? And is the mine battling both the mind and the Harvard Outline? Why is the mind aligned with the Harvard Outline? Or is the Harvard Outline just appended to the duel: mine vs. mind? So much confusion and this is just the title.

An outline is a technology designed to organize and clarify our thoughts, but Ander Monson never pretends that this one will. He writes:

> b. but I've never been comfortable with the thing…
>> i. never felt the top-down structuralist method constructing writing to be useful or effective; the mind so idiosyncratic, unusual

From the beginning we see a struggle, a writer pushing against a form he cannot abide. He eventually calls the outline "suspect" and through that accusation forces the outline to see itself, as if in a hall of mirrors:

> e. headings
>> i. subheadings
>>> 1. sub-subheadings

And in the mirrors the outline has no choice but to admit to its imperfections as it glitches:

       i. which called themselves
         1. which called themselves

And finally the outline breaks down and breaks the rules and moves against its own flow:

         2. and exited
       ii. right back
    c. out

By the end of the first page Monson has the outline dismantling itself, showing us the impossibility or, at least, the absurdity of attempting to standardize the expression of our thoughts or the structure of that expression. But instead of abandoning the flawed form, he does what any essayist must: he embraces the struggle. He writes on — outlines further — for eight pages. He investigates the form despite its imperfections and its inability to hold together. He revels in the bones:

    c. again that attraction to what elegance there is to find

Throughout section II, Monson's search for elegance focuses on industrial mining, his family's history with mining and how the technology of retrieving precious metals from the earth has left Upper Michigan full of ghost towns. There is not a single reference to the outline form in this section, but because Monson clings to the aesthetics of the form, even after dismantling its utility, we cannot help but compare the technology of the outline to the technology of the mine.

    b. though the shells they left behind — the fine network of tunnels that still riddle the earth — are havens for millions of bats

Monson writes of exploring the abandoned copper mines below the ghost towns of the Keweenaw Peninsula, but he might as well be exploring the used up shafts of the Harvard Outline itself. With every twist and turn and indent we understand more how the outline is maybe a destructive technology that endangers human expression in the same ways that mining endangers the towns of Upper Michigan. After all, both technologies privilege efficiency and standardization over patience and idiosyncrasy in the retrieval and handling of precious materials — copper in the mines and information in the outlines.

In section III, "The outline, so like a mine," Monson finally makes his comparison explicit. Both technologies are "defined by penetration," deeper into information or arguments and deeper into the earth. It is a sex joke, "you dirty bird," but it is a dark one. When has the earth ever consented to our penetration of it? Even the terminology of mining, Monson tells us, has this darkness in it:

> 2. and the aura of danger, of esoteric, academic secret knowledge about them
> a. they literally describe loci of danger, pits and sinkholes; they offer both treasure and death

So too does the form of the outline offer both treasure and death, the chance to discover something precious only to exploit it with the technology of the outline. Take, for instance, how Monson arrives at the death of his mother:

> i. so maybe the outline is a kind of architecture I am trying to erect
> ii. to protect myself against my family, meaninglessness, and the future
> 1. an artifice to get inside the past
> 2. like a cold and unlit hole — what family tragedy is there behind me glittering like a vein
> iii. perhaps it is a womb
> 1. and this then has to do with my mother's death
> 2. a protective sheath, a comfort zone
> iv. or it could be a shell
> b. an attempt for rigor as some buffer or protection
> c. or maybe it is elegance for the sake of it
> d. an infinite recursion
> e. some wankery

Here the burrowing form of the outline has led Monson to dig so deeply that he arrives unexpectedly at the pain of losing his mother, but then, exactly because of the form that led him there, the recognition of her death is immediately lost in a sub-

subheading, rushed past as the structure of the outline forces him onward before there is any chance for the kind of messy human response that might muck up the efficiency of the technology. The technology of the outline has indeed uncovered something precious, but it has stripped away patience and idiosyncrasy and with it, any chance at empathy. And in this moment the outline glitches once again, skips a beat; after heading "iv" there is no subheading "a" — as if in remembrance of what the technology has snuffed out.

On the page, this is almost unrecognizable as an essay, an outline devouring itself. It is a cannibal savagely adorned, wearing its meal, at times, like a trophy. But there is great elegance in the language, in the movement from academia to abandoned mines to family history. If Monson's essay sometimes enjoys the "wankery" of playing around inside the clunky cogs of the Harvard Outline, it is not out of regression but out of prescience and the attempt to startle us into understanding that ghost towns like those of the Keweenaw Peninsula may still arise and we may as well expect them to haunt us after the Information Age, just as they have haunted us after the Industrial Age.

The fear that lingers after "Outline . . . " is that imposing any "top-down structuralist method" (like the Harvard Outline or even Google) on our attempts to communicate information through writing might reduce our information to nothing more than a commodity that we churn out and use up rather than treasure. And so our communication of information — our nonfiction, our essays — must be patient and idiosyncratic and creative so that we are not left with abandoned tunnels, so that, as Monson warns, we are not left:

> 3. with no way of lighting up again, and no way
> iii. back out —

Joshua Wheeler: Toward the end of "Outline Towards a Theory..." you claim that you write in order "to protect myself against my family, meaninglessness, and the future." Nonfiction as protection against the future is maybe an uncommon definition. In what ways is the essay uniquely suited for engaging with the future?

Ander Monson: To essay is to engage in a very old behavior, but it's one that, by constant practice and the relative stability of the human brain over the centuries, can still feel familiar to us. If an essay is, as I believe, an artificial intelligence, then what better way to speak to the future than through it? Admittedly it's hard not to fear that the way we live and work and think is shifting somewhat — as it surely shifted in the past — and this is probably due to technology (even in the way that the shift from oral to written cultures changed our capacity for memory), so it's not a lock that the future will be able to still read our minds or run our code, but natural languages are far more forgiving than computer code, so it seems to me a pretty good bet that what we do here and now will still be decipherable — and maybe even timely.

JW: Essay as artificial intelligence? In your book, *Vanishing Point*, you call its essays, "...a kind of frozen thinking...a cheapo virtual reality." Do these all describe this specific essay?

AM: "Outline Towards a Theory..." moreso than most of my essays, consists pretty transparently of routines and subroutines, a hierarchical mode of thinking that I'm both engaging in therein and working against. Moreso than apparently formless prose (which, well, don't get me started on: all prose is formal in some way and hierarchical because syntax and meaning depend on hierarchy and form, etc.), the outline echoes and enacts a kind of analog and clunky programming language. That's why the form's so restrictive, and hence so pleasurable to work within in order to find its seams.

JW: When I read "Outline Towards a Theory . . . " in 2013, your references to Google, though brief, loom large. What is the danger of Google for the essayist?

AM: The major danger of the availability of search — and not just of Google — is the availability of an apparent (but powerfully uninfinite, on further study) infinity. For starters, any infinity is paralyzing. This is the job of the nonfiction writer: to take from what's available (which is everything) and to cut away swathes of vastness until what remains lights up a connection. Google cannot do that for you. And the larger the infinity the more difficult the task at hand. Algorithms and heuristics can get us a little ways, but they won't get us all the way, not yet. In a way we're better off with restrictions, with constraint. The human brain is designed for that, to function best in cramped quarters, when we're told what not to do or what we cannot do. Then we get inventive and something of us is revealed.

And besides it's not really an infinity at all. That is, it appears that everything is at our fingertips. But really it's a very small proportion of the available information that's in any way googleable. Try to find a minor murder trial from 1984. The world of Google search may not avail you, though they will probably note your interest somewhere in their records.

The vast majority of information isn't so easily recorded. Our lives have an exceptionally high bandwidth. What about an afternoon you spent a week ago — much less a decade ago — you know, with that one girl?

You see my point. Partly it paralyzes. Partly it's an illusion.

JW: So, as Joan Didion says, we have to write to find out what we know.

AM: I imagine that most of the essayists I love believe in some variation on that Didion quote. Everything's an experiment, and we do experiments because we don't completely know what the result will be. So every piece of writing is an opening, and not usually one that requires intention or planning, exactly, though everything before an essay's composition turns out in retrospect to be preparation for the essay that I'm writing at the moment.

My belief is that composition is like the scene in Cocteau's *Orpheus* where Orpheus listens to a car radio in dim light, receiving some kind of transmission. I'm not sure what kind of transmission I'm listening for, but I am listening.

THE PERIMETERS OF CHAOS

THE PERIMETERS OF CHAOS

THE PERIMETERS OF CHAOS

BARRET BAUMGART

INTERVIEW WITH MARY RUEFLE
BY BARRET BAUMGART

The word "paragraph," from the Greek *paragraphos*, means "written beside." I felt strange when I first learned this. What were paragraphs written beside? As I began to wonder, it seemed to me that the only possible answer was the writer herself. The pen covers the blank page and the writer sees written beside her, in an expanding block of prose, her own shadow unfurl. A paragraph is the murky workings of a mind projected in a moment of inspiration; it's an attempt to transpose the outlines of the self, to externalize one's interior in a magic outpouring of prose.

Or so I thought. Historically, such spontaneous overflowings are usually the province of poetry. Paragraphs, as it turns out, are not the substance of lyric possession, but units of logic, the basic building blocks of rationally grounded truths, which result in human agreements, in God and government, capitals and monuments, money and war. For most of written history, the paragraph was merely an ornate punctuation mark written beside a word to indicate the successful conclusion of an idea. The symbol, a *pilcrow*, looks like a backward *P*, but in actuality it's a *C* adorned with vertical lines: ¶. In an attempt to vivify the leaden prose of the philosophers, lords, and bishops who hired them, scribes adorned these *C*'s with wings and painted them red. The *C* stood for *capitulum*, "little head." These innumerable, small winged beings, paradoxically, represent the historic, bombastic pretensions of prose.

Although we still use paragraphs as visual tools to organize and delimit our ideas, today the convention of the pilcrow has been dropped. Nevertheless, whenever we read a lengthy paragraph we're reminded of prose's abiding big-headed ambitions. Beside the rapid line breaks of poetry, long paragraphs often appear like dreary projections of masculine megalomania; long afternoon shadows falling from capital city obelisks. And why shouldn't they? Prose is by definition prosaic — ordinary, commonplace, violent. But is poetry any less so?

Mary Ruefle is traditionally recognized as a poet, yet in some of her most influential works she is a prose writer. Her essay "Monument" is a single, justified 934-word-long block. Reading "Monument," despite its imposing appearance, one experiences the contradictory sense that Ruefle has projected the puzzled shadow of the contemporary human brain onto this dense block paragraph. In this way, her prose achieves the lyrical inspiration I wish existed in the etymology of the word paragraph — written beside. While "Monument" positions us before an imprisoning wall of prose, we find to our surprise that we are able to walk through that wall and into a shadow realm which refuses to transfer meaning or prescribe truth. Her paragraphs do not amount to a thesis but rather a perimeter, the confines of which her mind constantly crashes against. As we read, we recognize the danger of these repeated attempts. Flawed grammatically, full of faulty logic, Ruefle winds through a maze of syntax. Like an insect tracing the mortar lines between bricks, uncertain of its route and doubling back, we search the surface of a wall which is an idea we'll never quite grasp. At the end, we're never sure if we've understood the text's intentions, if we've surmounted or simply fallen off somewhere near the middle of the paragraph. Doubling back, we reread, gathering clues, tracing the lines of meaning. Eventually we run out of words and stand confused in Ruefle's shadow.

So is "Monument" a poem, an essay, something in between? I doubt whether Mary Ruefle is much inspired by such questions. In many ways, her work might be read as a monument to such petty and unfruitful genre wars. "A small war had ended," she writes in her opening lines. "Like all wars it was terrible." At the start of "Monument," Ruefle, or her persona, walks into a capital city park, sits on a bench and watches ducks frolic in a pond. She is happy for the chance to rest. She has been traveling in conjunction with the war, of which she was a "veteran architect," and now she must design a monument to commemorate the war, "that acre of conflagration" as she calls it. The essay abounds with consonance, as though with each recurrent crunching C-sound Ruefle is herself attempting to bite the head off her idea — that little capitulum — to escape conclusions. "I had entered the park aimlessly," Ruefle writes, "trying to escape my ideas." Indeed, Ruefle's numerous run-on sentences, her deliberate placement of commas where there should be periods, and the unfolding length of her single justified paragraph, all these underscore her speaker's need to extend beyond herself by pushing at the perimeters of the page. This movement is the key to why "Monument" works. Swept beneath the rapid momentum of the speaker's rising thought, the reader soon finds that, in Ruefle's hands, the paragraph no longer marks a unit of logic, but more, opens a violent "theater of conflict," as she says at one point. We watch the speaker kneel and outline an imaginary perimeter around an insect. Then, crossing toward a drinking fountain, she crushes it, along with any reader still waiting for a logically argued essay about the trauma of war.

"Above all I desired to be left in peace," the speaker says. But until the essay is finished, peace remains impossible. The speaker leans over a drinking fountain. An "arch" of clear water rises toward her lips. "I wanted to kiss it," she says. Is this ephemeral arch Ruefle's monument of triumph? The word *monument* is derived from the Latin *menere*, to remember — to warn. The etymology cautions me against trying to interpret. What remains certain, however, is that at bottom, "Monument" is about moving forward — surviving. To live is to gather momentum. To die is to build a monument. Ruefle swallows her water and walks on, recalling the meaning of the word *speculum*, which is "not only an instrument regarded by most with horror, but also a medieval compendium of all knowledge." *The Speculum Maius* (*Great Mirror*) written by the Dominican friar Vincent Beauvius in 12th century compiled all the world's knowledge in 4,000 chapters spanning 32 books. Beauvius composed each chapter in a single block paragraph only broken, periodically, by carefully painted pilcrows. But Ruefle tells us none of this. She must move forward. A speculum, she says, is also "a patch of color on the lower wing segments of most ducks." And it is the image of ruby-emerald bird wings that, like a dozen pairs of missing pilcrows, provides Ruefle's conclusion. She ends with ornate diction, a philosopher satisfied after having proven the existence of God: "Thus I was able, in serenest peace, to make my way back to my garret and design the memorial which was not elected and never built . . ."

Ruefle skillfully blends the historic bombastic appearance of prose with the ecstasy of poetic insight and then undercuts both approaches by refusing to grant us access to the nature of her revelation and the logical steps that precipitated its arrival. Yet rather than feeling frustrated, or that the speaker is being coy, we feel somehow uplifted, transformed. What Ruefle and her reader ultimately escape remains a mystery. But it doesn't matter. By the end of "Monument" our identification with the speaker is so complete that her sudden survival becomes our own: "I looked up ... saw the ducks in midflight, their wings shedding water drops which returned to the pond, and remembered in amazement that I could swallow, and I did..." We emerge from shadow into a shocking daylight clarity we cannot explain. In this way, in the passionate play between logic and lyric, light and shadow, Ruefle's work sidesteps the expectations of both prose and poetry. Pilcrows fly. Poetry crawls. And the reader delights. "Monument" is hardly an argument about paragraphs. It is, however, an obliteration of stagnation. Today a substantial portion of world's knowledge is available free on the Internet in paragraphs of prose. How will we handle this expanding imposition of certainty? How will we preserve the mystery on which art and life feed? The answer, as seen in Mary Ruefle's "Monument," lies in writing beside ourselves.

Barret Baumgart: "Monument," like the majority of your essays, includes no line or paragraph breaks. Do you consider these single unbroken prose units paragraphs? Is it important that your prose appear a certain way visually on the page?

Mary Ruefle: A prose piece of mine (for that's what I call them, "pieces") called "The Bench" was included in a textbook designed for first-year college students studying the ever-mandatory subject of composition. When my free copy arrived, I noticed that at the back of the book there were questions on each essay in the book, questions that were supposed to stimulate discussion. The first question on my piece was: Why didn't Ruefle use paragraphs? When I read that, I almost fell out of my chair laughing; I wished very much that I could be in the classroom, in the back of the room, and when the teacher asked why didn't Ruefle use paragraphs, I would raise my hand and give the only honest answer: It never occurred to her!

BB: Who is the speaker in "Monument?"

MR: The speaker in "Monument" is, presumably, an architect who is walking through a park in a capitol city after a war. I think of him as a male because so many architects for so long a time were male (I should be ashamed of my assumption). But beneath the architect there is me, who wrote the story sitting on a park bench in Washington, DC, after an intensely horrific finale of a romantic relationship.

BB: What is at stake, for the writer, in the decision to break a line or extend it into prose? How do you know which form your writing should take?

MR: I definitely think stories are better suited to prose. I very rarely tell stories in my poems, but I very often do in my prose. I determine the form (poetry or prose) in my ear — I literally hear either poetry or prose, I just here it, they have different sounds, different rhythms; poetry almost always doubles back on itself, two steps back for every step forward, while prose just keeps on going, full steam ahead. Of course this is very general, I am speaking in general, there are no rules, and no two ears are alike.

BB: Reading "Monument," we feel present at the climax of some profound emotional crisis, yet the speaker resists giving us ultimate access to the true nature of her dilemma, as well as to what eventually resolves it. Despite this fact, we still manage to share in the speaker's transformation. Can you explain the nature of this effect?

MR: When I write, I don't think much about what I am writing, I am simply trying to alleviate an intense pressure inside my head, I have described it like having to pee, only in your head. I cannot explain the nature of the effect, but perhaps it is that the reader has felt the pressure, too, and that it has been alleviated for me, so it has been alleviated for the reader. I do not think I have held anything back from the reader, at least not on purpose. When I sat down on the park bench that afternoon in Washington, DC, I was agitated, and when I stood up I was peaceful; I have not held that back from the reader, and that is the only thing that matters. That is the important thing, that is the Truth of the matter, everything else is irrelevant.

BB: How is the essay construed broadly throughout the United States today? Do you think the umbrella term "lyric essay" helps or hinders *Seneca Review*'s ambitions? Do you consider "Monument" a lyric essay?

MR: Certainly *Seneca Review* was instrumental in widening the field of what we loosely call nonfiction. They were brave and influential in that, and so I think they have reached their goal, but every achievement has a variety of effects; for instance, there is a great deal of crazy, unfocused nonfiction being written today, and there is now nothing that can stop it — be careful for what you wish! I think the essay today, as a concept and form, is much wider than it was thirty years ago, but a lot of that has to do with postmodernism and the breakdown of borders. Is a snowboard a skateboard or a ski? Is "Monument" a lyric essay? I don't know, it kinda reads to me like a story. I have written things since that are much more essayistic, in which the speaker is clearly myself writing on a specific subject. But when I wrote "Monument," I had not really written much prose in a very long time — as any fool can see, it never even occurred to me to use paragraphs!

EXPERIMENTS

EXPERIMENTS

EXPERIMENTS

EXPERIMENTS

EXPERIMENTS

MICHAL MILSTEIN

INTERVIEW WITH
GENEVIEVE TURKETT
BY LISA GRAY GIURATO

"If your daughter is going to get through life," Mr. H told my mother, "she is going to have to learn how to think like a scientist."

I was failing sixth-grade Life Sciences. Mr. H called my parents every Friday to report my weaknesses: I hadn't memorized a thing, I couldn't stay on task, I rarely finished my homework, and when I did complete an assignment my lab reports were usually dreadful. He explained that these reports were designed to force me to prove or disprove an idea, to help me employ logic and then replicate the process for another reader. The experiment's subject didn't matter. Flora, fauna, prisoners, angels — no matter the specimen, the concept stayed the same: something is true if all its parts are true and stay true, even in someone else's hands.

In theory, the lab report leaves no room for subjectivity. In practice, however, subjectivity is inevitable. Genevieve Turkett didn't write "Bodily Violence" to reflect on the nature of truth (both capital "T" and lowercase "t"). Instead, her essay demonstrates how tired and senseless the "truth" argument is. By mimicking the processes we use to attain knowledge, "Bodily Violence" reveals the sacrifices — the "redactions" — we make in order to achieve the illusion of Truth.

There are two texts in "Bodily Violence," one that observes and one that discovers. The unmarked text aims for objectivity. It's a pedagogical tool for conducting future experiments. But it is also a violent degradation of a horrific emotional experience; it is removed from both the pain of the tragedies its supposedly about and the prevention of them. It observes, but it does not witness.

If you combine the small fragments of redacted text, you will see that they systematically fit together to form coherent paragraphs. Combine the redacted parts in the "Introduction" and you'll have:

> ~~It was raining that day, slightly and persistently on the long windows. He didn't mean it. Maybe he didn't mean it. It was just his growing up. It was unbearable.~~

Do it again for the text in "Materials and Methods":

> ~~Tell the whole truth and nothing but the truth. He was just a kid. There's something he wasn't saying. Don't push, she told us in kindergarten. Something feels sick, those bars of light through the windows slashing at my fingers. No one every paid attention to me...~~

These are not observations. They are emotional discoveries of unthinkable loss, human reactions to the backwater data that inundates the rest of the page. They witness. These redactions are where Turkett's essay truly exists, far from the lab report's sterile tone. They are the bits and pieces of mold on the agar, the undistilled water, the titrations that are one drip over the limit. They are what a science teacher would call "contaminations."

But they are not the whole essay. Both texts, redacted and preserved, rely on each other to form Turkett's remarkable essay. Initially, I asked myself which text was more "true," and then I realized that trying to answer that question would be a disservice to the essay. "Bodily Violence" is about the miracle of being able to observe and witness at the same time, not about revealing a shrouded truth. Turkett shows the dualities of our minds, the conflicts that drive a person to become an essayist. "Bodily Violence" is about the experience of writing through dualities, futilities, and revelations, and it asserts that in order to get through life, we need to think more like essayists.

Lisa Gray Giurato: So, after reading your essay, I was curious if your profession was in the sciences and that's why you choose to write an essay that critiques the clinical voice found in scientific jargon?

Genevieve Turkett: I was a creative writing minor in college and wrote all the time, but now being a public school teacher, it's tough to find the time to write. At the time I wrote the essay, I was reading research studies about very emotional subjects — abuse, poverty, hunger, psychological trauma. The juxtaposition between the emotionally charged subject matter and the cold scientific jargon seemed anachronistic, as if a temporal distance was created through the language itself from the emotional reality of the people involved in these traumatic events.

LGG: I can see why you were drawn to teaching. What do you teach?

GT: English, in a low-income and high-risk area where the reading levels of my students in a senior English course can range from a 1st-grade reading level to a 12th-grade reading level.

LGG: What role do you see the literary essay playing in secondary education today? Do you teach the literary essay, and what are your students reading?

GT: I think the literary essay can play a bigger role in secondary education in the future. Teaching novels gets harder and harder — you have to buy the books for the students, many of them struggle with longer works, and teaching Shakespeare and Steinbeck becomes difficult. Literary essays are interesting and different for students, and they're *shorter*.

LGG: Besides the accessibility to readers, why do you think teaching students to write the literary essay is helpful?

GT: Students can learn to write their own, whereas writing a novel in class is not possible at all.

LGG: So the shorter form makes it, pedagogically speaking, an easier form to teach. In what other ways, is the length helpful?

GT: Teachers can print essays unlike novels. Trust me, I had to print a class set of *The Great Gatsby* last year. It was *not cheap*. It's time that as English teachers, we branch out from what we were taught in school and look at other options. It's not the end of the world if a kid graduates without ever reading the classics. It's tough for us to accept that those works are less useful these days, and it pains us because we see the classic novels as akin to some form of spirituality, but it's a truth we have to accept. When your students can't read and books scare them and their whole family, a cool, experimental, interesting literary essay can change the way they look at reading.

LGG: I've read that the Common Core State Standards advocate for a greater emphasis on reading nonfiction in general with a push for a diversity of forms, such as the essay, but also podcasts, photographic essays, and journalism. With such a wide diversity of form within nonfiction, how has the Common Core State Standards influenced the way the literary essay and nonfiction is taught in the classroom?

GT: I'm in the minority of teachers these days that *love* the CCSS. The idea of standardizing expectations across the country will make our jobs as educators easier in the long run, though right now it's scaring the crap out of most of us.

LGG: Why aren't you scared off?

GT: I don't find it that scary because the CCSS is so broad you can fit almost anything into it. Literature has a place in the English classroom of course, but English teachers can cling to their Hemingway the way Tea Partiers cling to the Constitution — that it can do no wrong, can never be changed, and to speak otherwise is heresy. If anything, CCSS gives more of a chance to the literary essay than current standards might, which emphasizes novels and short stories that have been done into the ground. I mean, if I have to teach *A Rose for Emily* one more time I might burn the damn thing.

LGG: So, what you're saying is that the many forms of the essay can seem fresh to students but provide a rich and broad mountain to mine for educators?

GT: New ideas and forms are important to teach, and with more nonfiction being taught in the classroom, there is less time to teach novels, but that's okay, because it means more space for the literary essay. Our students are our future employees and employers, innovators and creators, they need to see a variety of formal possibilities, and that means that the classic forms might need to get taught less often. It won't kill us, I promise.

NOURISHMENT

NOURISHMENT

NOURISHMENT

NOURISHMENT

NOURISHMENT

MICHAL MILSTEIN

INTERVIEW WITH WENDY WALTERS
BY MICHAL MILSTEIN

In "Chicago Radio," there is too much water and too little to eat. Its subjects are water-boarded and starved. Prisoners are malnourished, mothers can't find fresh food, a man's garden is uprooted and replaced with canned vegetables. Swimmers hallucinate, a plane is lost in a storm, a brother drowns, slaves drown themselves. It's the story of people who are both inundated and overlooked. The refrains of the radio DJ and his callers resemble cries in the dark, conversations between sufferers and their god, a being who chaotically grants wishes and denies prayers.

The emotional journey to the essay's center is as complex as its structure. On my first read, "Chicago Radio" seemed fundamentally disjointed, an intriguing collage without essayistic intention, as if Walters had taken pieces from different puzzles and shuffled them together. I'd find a pattern, and then a piece with a different cut and design would spoil the system.

Supermarkets and vegetable patches go together, I thought, *and drowned slaves and brothers make sense, but how do all of these things come together? Do they have the same theme? Do they have the same feeling?*

Yes, my first read was primarily analytical, but that's what first reads are: they position the essay in a logical structure, prepping the mind for future readings. An essay's framework is made up of the interlocking parts of an argument. So, what makes us return to the same essay over and over again? It certainly isn't the argument itself. If that were the case, we would simply abandon an essay after its argument — its promise — was fulfilled.

"Chicago Radio" forces its readers to reexamine and re-expose themselves to beautiful, seemingly disparate images in order to construct their own argument. By inviting the reader to draw his or her own associations between vitamin supplements and UFO sightings, grocery stores and drowning victims, eardrums and cemetery gardens, Walters pressures us to become parts of a noisy clamor, pieces of an unexplainable history that can only be described in scraps. We become emotional witnesses; the moment we draw meaningful connections between the essay's pieces is the moment we become participants and enactors implicated in the act of storytelling and essaying itself. Their story becomes our story.

One might ask: Isn't it primarily the job of the essayist, and not the reader, to elucidate unseen connections, to form a clear and enduring argument? Is "Chicago Radio" just an abstraction, a random, subconscious cry in the dark? The central theme of this essay, even beyond violence and racial inequality, is defenselessness, and Walters enacts this theme with her form. By making the connections of her essay partially dependent on an outsider's mind, Walters makes her art — and herself — vulnerable. It's this act itself, and not the thematic interdependence of the sections themselves, that makes "Chicago Radio" an essay instead of a novelty; Walters argues that in order to write about humiliation and vulnerability, the essayist must make his or her essay vulnerable as well. Of course, all great writing should leave room for interpretation and draw on the idiosyncratic experiences of its readers, but "Chicago Radio" is exceptional because it completely abandons the urge to dictate.

This doesn't mean that "Chicago Radio" can't survive without the inferences of its readers. On subsequent readings I asked myself why Walters chose this structure, why she felt that continents of disparate texts needed to exist next to each other to create a world, her world, the geography of racial inequality. And then I realized that the artistry — and the argument — of this essay exists in the friction between these continents of words, how they collide and drift apart. It made me believe that, at one time, all of "Chicago Radio's" sections (and the personal histories of blacks in America) existed together in some sort of Pangaea (or Walter's "Drexciya"), and were violently ripped apart by that same force that drowns and starves children in the ghetto. The essay argues that if experiences of racial inequality are never unified in narrative, then victims will remain powerless, their memories drifting apart toward infinity.

Michal Milstein: I understand that "Chicago Radio" was originally published as a poem. Our committee, however, chose to call it a lyric essay. Does this designation change the meaning of the work for you?

Wendy Walters: At the time I was frustrated that lot of my poems had been rejected for being too long, so I wrote "Chicago Radio" as a kind of affirmation of my personal aesthetics without any expectation that I could publish it first in a journal. The lyric essay seems very American to me, not just in content but in form — it was an unprecedented performance of indirect associations, the art of talking slant. I appreciated and could relate to that kind of work on a very deep level. So, when the editors designated my piece a lyric essay, how I thought about the work didn't change, but I did, for a moment, feel understood as a writer.

MM: Why do you feel a deep connection with the essay? Or, why did it help you feel understood?

WW: I felt like I was not alone in thinking that it was more important for me to try to say what I wanted to say than to stick to expectations of genre.

MM: I also am interested in knowing how you went about your research for this project. There was some found text (the DJ records), but other sections seem to be miracles in their own rights, as if they appeared out of nowhere.

WW: Miracles are always appearing, right? The challenge, at least for me, is how to make sure I notice them. The story about vitamins in prisons was reported by several news outlets one week, and I kept thinking about it. I heard the report about "food deserts" in Detroit on the radio when I was there visiting family.

The piece struck me because when I lived downtown during the late 1990s, I did not understand why there were so few grocery stores in the city. At the time I wrote this piece, I was single and living in Providence. I spent a lot of evenings listening to the radio — every night someone seemed to be sharing an amazing account of devotional endurance. I overheard the conversation about the proposal while driving home late from a work event. I think I was also in my car when I heard the conversation about the young parents not getting along. I invented the other two DJ conversations from details in my own family history, but since the piece wasn't about me, I didn't note them as such.

MM: "...But the piece wasn't about me." This is a beautifully woven essay, and I can't help but think that part of it is about you. Am I completely wrong?

WW: Thanks for that. And you aren't completely wrong. I would say the essay is personal in that it reveals my preoccupations and efforts at connecting them. The associations reveal how I understand things — or how I understood them during the time I was composing the piece. I am the DJ. But the essay is not about me explicitly — meaning for the most part, it is not an account of incidents in my life.

MM: That's fascinating. I feel like each section is its own stanza to a song. How do you think these sections talk (or interact) with each other? Is this essay a playlist, or on shuffle? What happens in the spaces in between each section?

WW: I wouldn't say the essay is a music shuffle, because I spent a lot of time arranging the order — though that order probably reflects the way I was thinking about the world at the time and not some resolute sense of proportion or architecture. That is to say, if I was writing the essay now, I might have chosen a different order.

The argument of this essay is that disparate realities are connected by the fact that they exist in the same moment. People who never encounter each other can share in an experience. All of the characters in "Chicago Radio" are engaged in the act of listening, which for me is one of the best ways to avoid being distracted by one's own feelings and history when pursuing a connection with someone else. I hope the gaps between the sections encourage the reader to listen better, to look for associations where otherwise they might have missed them.

ELIOT WEINBERGER
AND THE MUSIC OF FACT

ELIOT WEINBERGER
AND THE MUSIC OF FACT

LAWRENCE YPIL

INTERVIEW WITH ELIOT WEINBERGER
BY SUZANNE CODY

In "An Archeology of Dreams [The North, c. 1000]" by Eliot Weinberger, we get annals of a different sort: not the account of battle, but of dreams. It offers not a list of lands conquered, deaths, the typical stuff of history, bodies strewn across a battlefield in broad daylight, but a chronicle of dreams: visions a king or a soldier might have had lying under the sky the night before a war is won.

> Þorbjörg of Indriðastaðir dreamed that eighty wolves passed by with flames coming from their mouths, and among them was a white bear.

> Glaumvör dreamed that a bloody sword was sticking out from her husband's tunic, and that a river ran through the house, sweeping away all their things.

> Hersteinn Blund-Ketilsson dreamed he saw his father on fire.

One-third of a three-part essay on Iceland ("Island"), "An Archaeology of Dreams" collects the dreams of characters that Weinberger encounters in the Icelandic sagas. Accounts of the tenth and eleventh century, the sagas were written in the thirteenth and fourteenth centuries and it is these documents that Weinberger scours for dreams and shapes into essays. He insists that he merely gathers and arranges these historical details, that he never invents them. But to consider Weinberger as a mere "collector" is misleading. Facts become like musical notes on a page, in Weinberger's hand — shaped, arranged, then set to music.

If "Archeology" reads like a poem, it's due to the essay's incantatory form. One dream happens after another, as in a series of utterances, which Weinberger weaves instinctively like verses in a song. Bypassing interpretation and commentary, Weinberger allows the images to speak for themselves in a rhythmic accumulation. A tongue so long it wound around his neck. A body stuffed with brushwood. A falcon with all its feathers plucked out.

If there is a "voice" in "Archeology," it is generated by an almost vibratory motion between passages. It is a lyric presence suggested by virtue of the curatorial: the mind at work moving through history. Or is it the ear? One easily imagines Weinberger leaning over the pages of the sagas as if he were listening to a radio station on the frequency of deep time.

> Þorkell Eyjólfsson dreamed his beard was so large it covered the land.

> Þorgils Orrasbeinsstjuper dreamed he looked at his knee, and five leeks were growing out of it.

> Þorgils Boovarsson dreamed that a tall woman came to his door, wearing a child's cloak, and she was very sad.

This mode of nonfiction is something that can be seen in many of Weinberger's essays, especially the ones that appear in *An Elemental Thing*. In "Changs," for example, Weinberger explores Chinese history and collects the lifestories of people who shared the same name (Chang): a kind of series of epitaphs that attest to what one can do with one's life. In "Wind," he gathers the words that share the same character (Feng) and establishes a web of associations between disparate things. In the process, the essay becomes a meditation on art, especially since we find out that the Chinese word for poet is composed of "wind" and "man."

In "Archaeology," by plumbing the depths of Iceland's history of dreaming, Weinberger, sentence by sentence, moves as in a vertical descent into the archives. Like a cross-section through time and space, "Archeology" allows the chronology of history, its past tense, to give way to the immanence and the present tense of simultaneity: not many dreamers but one. Where the essay form these days so conveniently slips into the thin strata of the self, the myopic view of yesterday and last month and "my life," Weinberger reclaims the possibility of the essay as a collective form. Perhaps this form is the closest contemporary correlative we have to the epic. A multiplicity of voices becomes a communal song. The dreams of Kostbera, Þorkell Eyjólfsson, Þorgils Örrasbeinsstjúper, all of them, becomes ours.

Suzanne Cody: You often begin your essays with a question. What question began this essay?

Eliot Weinberger: I have an essay about tigers that began when I wondered: When Blake wrote "Tyger, Tyger," had he ever seen a real tiger? That led onto a trail of tiger beliefs and myths through various cultures to the near-extinction of tigers today. My essay "The Falls" began with two questions — began as two essays — that then started intertwining: Why did the Nazis believe they were Aryans, those brown-skinned people in India? And, in the Rwanda genocide, why did the Hutus think the Tutsis were the descendants of Shem, one of Noah's sons? This resulted in a long collage of moments from some 4,000 years of racism.

I've always been attracted to questions because — apart from imperatives — they are the only sentences that are neither true nor untrue. They are like a line of poetry.

But this particular essay did not begin with a question. It began with reading and with traveling. It's just a little homage to Icelandic culture.

SC: I've heard that your only rule in writing nonfiction is that all information must come from documented sources.

EW: That's true. I'm a pre-pomo, otherwise known as a modernist, so I have the old-fashioned belief that an essay should not include fictional elements — not in the sense that they are "true," but rather in the sense that someone other than the author believes them to be true. Otherwise, the essay strikes me as largely unexplored territory, and, like fiction or poetry, without limitations of form or content.

SC: So, working on the assumption that all these dreams are documented, can you tell me about how you found them and, particularly, why you felt that this form would be the best way to essay about them? What influences came into play (from Icelandic culture or not) in the creation of "Archaeology?"

EW: In the '90s I made a number of trips to Iceland, which coincided with the publication of a magnificent five-volume edition of the complete Icelandic sagas. The sagas are not mythological, but the stories of the real people who settled Iceland around the year 1000, and they seem to me models of how narrative could be written. They are, in almost all ways, the opposite of the bourgeois novel. It is pure storytelling, without long descriptive passages, without nuances of emotional states (but not without indirect psychological insight), without metaphor or simile-based "good writing," and so on. Their sentences are as hard as rocks, and I've learned a lot from them.

All of the dreams in this little essay are taken directly from the sagas. The details are the same, but I've rewritten them; it's not cut and paste. I like dreams as an entry into a culture. We're all human; we all dream the same kinds of dreams. But the specifics of these dreams are, of course, quite different. They are mysterious snapshots from other worlds.

SC: Were those sagas in translation, or did you do the translations? I am always interested in how translation affects meaning, and what is lost in the process.

EW: I don't know Icelandic. In other essays, I translate some bits myself, or adapt existing translations. But the cliché of "lost in translation" is, unlike many clichés, not necessarily true. A lot is gained in translation. There are countless small felicities where one can do something in the translation-language that could not be done in the original. Most important of all, there is the invention of a new music, one that didn't exist in the original. And, of course, through the transformations of translations, one "gains" readers for the text.

SC: How would you define the lyric essay? Do you feel it can be defined?

EW: The "lyric essay" is a very recent but until it has been more concretely defined or further elaborated by its proponents, and practiced as such, one can't assume that it exists. I understand that "lyric essay" is meant to be something different than the traditional essay, which is a first-person, nonfictional narrative or rumination that proceeds in a linear fashion. But many of the pieces of writing labeled as "lyric essay" seem to me to be precisely that.

However debased the term "avant-garde" may be, perhaps we should think of "avant-garde essays," since the essay form, unlike poetry or fiction, has never had an avant-garde in English. "Avant-garde," to keep it short, could be defined as "something *The New Yorker* would never dream of publishing."

Or perhaps we should think of the "epic essay" . . . not in terms of length or scope or pretension, but as a repository of things a culture knows, not presented in the first person. It's the original function of the epic.

SC: Why do you see "Archaeology" as essay?

EW: Well, why not? It's not fiction, obviously. It's not poetry, though it looks a little like poetry, because it is not a product of my imagination, except very indirectly. It's nonfiction in that these are the real dreams of real people. So why not call it an essay? Or, more exactly, why isn't it an essay?

IN THE PRESENT TENSE

IN THE PRESENT TENSE

IN THE PRESENT TENSE

IN THE PRESENT TENSE

SUZANNE CODY

INTERVIEW WITH SHAWN WEN
BY SUZANNE CODY

Marcel Marceau as Bip is a protean man. A twist of white across the black stage: Bip the fireman, Bip the lion tamer, Bip the soldier. Bip commits suicide, takes the train, flies to the moon. Bip attends a fancy party, rides the subway, is chased by a bumblebee. Bip the forger with his ink and crayons. Bip the hero leading children over the mountains. Each identity is specific, precise, and yet also malleable — transitions seamless, one absolute melting into another, no spaces between. But Bip never speaks, his performance a silent essay enacted in the present tense.

The lyric tends toward the present tense — it may refer to a past event, but the thoughts and emotions exist in the now. Not: *this is how I felt*, but instead: *this is how I feel*, the immediacy allowing the audience to assume the predicament of the other, without the safe buffer of time passed.

Shawn Wen's "Parts of the Body," fuses lyric with essay in an attempt to fill the silence left by Marceau's uncompleted autobiography — perhaps unfinished because, as Wen notes, Marceau the performer never found words to be enough. Or else, like Proteus, Marceau refused to give up his truths to anyone who could not capture him.

When an actor, like Marceau, creates a character, he first outlines the given circumstances of that character — details gleaned from the text of the play, or from outside research. Even in the silence of mime, this is important — creation never occurs in a void. To mime a fireman, one must know something about what firemen do. The list — which might include, for example, that the character was a shy boy who nonetheless loved to perform, or that he was a young Jewish man living in Europe during World War II, or that he used his hands as he spoke — helps the actor form a deeper understanding of the character, provides a room to inhabit full of small telling objects, clues, secrets. This is not the sexy work of acting, all lights and applause, but the hidden part, the scaffolding containing a character.

In "Parts of the Body," Marcel Marceau is the character, with Wen cataloging the given circumstances for us. Comments by critics, the contents of his house, a table of countries he toured. Marriages, divorces, his own observations of himself: "'I was not the greatest father. I was too busy flying around the world.'" Intimacies: in the loveliest moment in the essay, Marceau encounters Charlie Chaplin, his childhood idol and inspiration, in an airport in Paris: "He approached Chaplin. And after talk of the weather, Marceau began to imitate the Little Tramp. Then Chaplin imitated Marceau's Little Tramp. Marceau brought his knees to the ground, took the Tramp's hand in his own, and kissed it. He looked up to see Chaplin's cheeks wet with tears."

Interspersed throughout this manifest of detail we find Wen coaxing us onto the stage where the play is already in progress.

> The applause begins before he steps onstage
> A white figure in the black deep
> White
> Because it shows movement
> White
> Because it hides the wrinkles
> White
> Because we are frail
> White
> The anguished, drawn-on lines of his face
> The face of a clown

Shifting out of the past of given circumstances and into the lyric present of the stage ("The applause begins — "), Wen invites us into "Parts of the Body," into the present tense of the character Marceau. For a moment, we witness his body painted white to show movement, white to hide wrinkles — and then "he" becomes "we" and the embodiment is complete: *he* is not frail, *we* are frail. As Wen has constructed the scaffolding of endless detail to capture our protean Marceau, it is a frailty we can assume in our own bodies, one we can know intimately. We are the actors and Wen is the director, guiding us in our brief possession. Then we shift away again, and "the anguished, drawn-on lines" are something we see, not suffer.

Throughout the essay we continue to move between past and present, but *we* becomes *you*. Relegated to the audience, we watch Bip kill a bull, struggle against the wind, walk a tightrope —

close, but not inside. For only a moment, we taste the success of the lyric, actors on the stage. But in the essay, Wen admits, we are still at the mercy of the written word: "…it's just a word," she says. "It can't dance. It can't run. It can't fall. You can read it. You can do so much as to pro-nounce it. Try to taste the sibilants as you tap your tongue against your teeth. But you still lack the shape and presence of a body." The writer of a lyric essay can build a cage around a protean man, but our intimacy is limited. Words are not enough to hold him.

Suzanne Cody: I'm interested in the history of "Parts of a Body" as a radio documentary — was it originally written with that intent?

Shawn Wen: Yes, the Marceau project started as a little joke — "mime radio." I wanted to see how audio could be used to describe something purely visual like mime. Audio producers like to say that radio is the most visual medium, because radio calls upon the imagination. The camera can only show what's exposed to the lens. But radio can go anywhere. Listeners automatically fill in the images in their minds. That's where this project was originally headed.

Marceau called his work "the art of silence." So the documentary was operating in accord with John Cage's idea that there's no such thing as silence. I went to Paris and Berlin to meet Marceau's former students. I made audio recordings of mime performances, zeroing in on the sound of breath, footsteps, clothes rustling, audience chatter. And I interviewed Marceau's students, calling on their own memories of working with their teacher.

I started digging through the archives at the New York Performing Arts Library, and I found Marceau's own voice in print — newspaper articles with quotes from him. His speech was grandiose, articulate, and flowery. It just had to be in the essay. But the idea of staging a reading of his words as an audio performance was so unappealing to me — it felt stilted. His words, as he spoke them, were such a direct link to him. Such an insight. And finding a voice actor to embody it seemed to dilute what I was trying to do with the work. In the end, that kind of killed the radio documentary. But it became a big push to create a more ambitious written piece.

SC: What do you feel writing in this form, rather than a simple narrative, brought to the documentary? Did it work the way you intended? Or if it didn't, what was the issue?

SW: This piece was never intended as a simple narrative. There was too much contradiction surrounding Marceau. In theater, was he a revolutionary or a cliché? Did he love to talk, or did he spurn it? The essay doesn't explain Marceau, so much as it wrestles with him. It's one of the freedoms that lyric essays lend their writers.

SC: Marcel Marceau once said, "Words are not enough." How do you think the form of the essay facilitated the creation of a work of words that would be "enough" to describe the man?

SW: A paradox lies at the heart of "Parts of a Body." How do you use language to describe mime? I agree with Marceau. Words are inadequate here. But words have their own movement, their own shape and gesture. I don't think they are "enough" to describe a man. But the words create something new.

Throughout the essay, Marceau taunts spoken and written language. I like that tension. He's almost stepping out of the page to insult the reader, and me, the writer.

SC: You said in your essay, "Then the writer is just a wannabe actor..." So instead of being writers, maybe we should all be actors?

SW: I don't think that all writers want to be actors. For one, I don't want to be an actor, but I am mesmerized by them. Actors must physically inhabit their craft. Their work lives in their bodies. You could argue that writers are impoverished by comparison, that they only put words on a page, and words can only *describe*. But I don't believe that. The text is a performance on a page. Text is more than a description. Text also summons a sensory experience. You know what I mean? Words have sound and shape. Words against other words create texture. Words ring in your head. They command images and emotions. So in reading and writing, we experience the text in ways that are physical as well as abstract.

And writing is a continuous improvisation.

SC: So, the lyric essay. What *is* a lyric essay?

SW: Traditional news, which is much of what I do now, functions to inform, but the lyric essay needs to drive itself. Not to say that the lyric essay doesn't inform. Readers likely leave an essay knowing more than before they came to it. But lyric essays flirt with their readers in a way that newspaper articles don't. A lyric essay can make an argument, or not. It can be playful, it can be pretty, it can be cagey, leaving a lot unsaid. I think lyric essays shine in moments where the writing is elliptical and certain details remain absent — readers are drawn to that evasiveness. In such a spare form, what you exclude is as important as what you include.

I take extensive notes. I love to cherry-pick facts. And ultimately, I see essaying as sculpting information. But I come to lyric essays to witness craft. Essaying is "sculpting information," and I love to see what other writers do with information — information that may be classified as "fact," or may be more ambiguous — when they give themselves the same freedoms of poets and novelists.

CECI NE PAS UNE LISTE

CECI NE PAS UNE LISTE

CECI NE PAS UNE LISTE

CECI NE PAS UNE LISTE

G. V. DE CHOISY

INTERVIEW WITH JOE WENDEROTH
BY G. V. DE CHOISY

Where does one start a list? At the beginning, of course — but where is that?

In the beginning, writing dealt in lists. The earliest writing we know of — anonymous Sumerian texts from around 4000 to 3500 B.C.E. — handled legal affairs. They were mostly finance and trade records, and marriage certificates — another sort of marketplace contract. These texts suggested steps to take if you were purchasing a donkey, or instructions you should follow to secure a warrantee on a wife.[1] Later, in Mesopotamia, the so-called List of Ziusudra proffered existential musings in bullet-pointed doses.[2]

That is how lists work. They are civilized and civilizing things. It is their job to look forward and to move their readers in the orderly direction of a positive future. And because lists accrue (especially if they are enumerated), they suggest a motion toward a finish that will be, ideally, larger than its start. This is no small thing that lists promise, and yet, it's a promise we trust them to keep.

I have learned not to trust Joe Wenderoth's lists. He has published two in *Seneca Review*, "69 Restrictions," which is included in this anthology, and "Things to Do Today," which is not. Both are fantastic, but I prefer talking about the former for the same reason I backed its inclusion in this collection. "69 Restrictions," quite simply, is a wolf in list's clothing.

What do I mean by that? Well, here is another thing that lists do. Not always, but often, the point of a list is to comfort. Even if their topic is no more serious than groceries, lists afford us the cushioning illusion that their subjects can be coped with if we just take the time to summarily reduce them, and line them up in rows. A list's accommodating form suggests its

---

[1] Or a divorce from one — not all business ventures are built to last, after all.

[2] Its ultra-modernized title, if anyone wants to plagiarize it in a blog post, could be "20 Ways to Rebuild Your Life After a Flood Destroys the Known World."

content is equally approachable: that certain lacks, personal or material, can be approached like triage; that emotional defects can be surmounted by organization; that major life goals can be accomplished, and then crossed out, as easily as if one were running a line through a completed errand.

Ostensibly, "69 Restrictions" is a contract, but no one in his or her right mind would consent to its terms. This contract is a list of odious impositions, the kind of contract that's forced on hesitant parties in the dark of night and signed in blood with a Montblanc pen. "69 Restrictions" is a numbered set of criteria — in actions to be taken, and opinions to be held — that dictates whether or not any "person shall be provided with genitalia."

It doesn't get much more personal than that. Look, the horrible thing about *The Metamorphosis* was not that Gregor Samsa woke up as a cockroach, but that he realized he was an animal.[3] This is disquieting territory, home to truths we prefer domesticated, but here's the thing: the wild things, the wolves Wenderoth has dressed like lists, are us. Consider Wenderoth's 38th restriction, in which we are obliged to demonstrate, "without a word (as in charades), the very real difference between the womb and the farm." A certain portion of our humanity is animality — that sociosexual part of ourselves we cannot fence in very well or for long. There's an upside to this. After all, as animals we get to reproduce with our genitalia. On the discomforting downside, we *have* to use our genitalia to reproduce.[4]

Wenderoth's lists don't care about your comfort. The standard enumeration in "69 Restrictions" does not soothe, and if it escalates to anything it is to a futile point of nauseating limits, an open prairie traded for a fenced grazing pasture, the final restriction being "the spirit of hampered freedom in general." And the concision of each numbered restriction in no way conveys or assures us that its content is manageable. Their terms are unbearable, in fact, and many of them are contradictory and unmanageable in the extreme.[5] Faced with Wenderoth's impossible set of conditions, we are doomed. We are all but guaranteed exactly what we do not want — a lack of genitalia — and that scenario's very probable consequences: less sex, fewer children, and an increase in isolation.

---

[3] Ditto: *Planet of the Ape*'s punch line.

[4] Barring the creative employment of petri dishes.

[5] There's the repulsive 35th restriction, for instance: "said person owns a vehicle made entirely of deceased family," or the coyly apocalyptic 63rd: "said person is conspicuously without blame with regard to the specific course taken by that which resists extinction almost successfully."

Is there a surer definition of tragedy than that: isolation, increased? Doubtful. But what's our alternative? Comedy, certainly, is not the opposite of tragedy, but its complement. If tragedy is an increase in isolation (especially one caused by a lack of genitalia), then its consequence will be a scarcity of life. What then? Think of the 1968 movie *Yours, Mine, and Ours*. Lucille Ball says to Henry Fonda, "You have ten children? I have eight!" Grocery bills be damned, Lucy and Henry get hitched and have kiddo number 19. This is comedy: life, increased.

And this is what Wenderoth does. He isolates us, and he increases life. And life, in Wenderoth's lists, is neither pure sorrow nor a total joke, but messy, ecstatic tragicomedy.[6] This is his 32nd restriction: "said person" must want to "live, if by 'live' one means resonate with difficulty." Wenderoth magnifies that difficulty, and in doing so, reveals its rewards. He renders human life and us, the lucky/poor bastards living it, in a grandiose form. He zooms in tight on our sad, funny, ugly, scabby, complementary, contradictory, inconsistent gorgeousness and he says, Here is living! Here is your junk! Here is your means to ultimate intimacy, and look how orderly I've made it for you. Look how neat, and look how clean. But remember, he also says, that order is an imposition, and oftentimes impossible.

Imagine how awful things would be if that weren't true. Imagine how boring. Imagine how restrictive.

---

[6] You know, the way life actually, mostly, is.

G. V. de Choisy: We've anthologized "69 Restrictions" as an essay, but you published a later version of it in a book of poems. Does it fit both categories?

Joe Wenderoth: Well, there's no way that I could argue that "69 Restrictions" is a poem. Not that I'd ever feel the need to. In most poetry books, you know, you're free to put in whatever you want. The points is: there's not some rule that says "Oh, you're making a book of poems? Then only poems in here!" What's the advantage to that restriction?

GVC: What's the disadvantage?

JW: Well, the question I think really is a question of the difference between fiction and nonfiction. I think. Or the Aristotelian idea, the difference between the probable and the possible.

GVC: The probable-impossible versus the improbable-possible?

JW: Yeah, that. As far as genre, well... you're in a nonfiction MFA program, right?

GVC: That's right.

JW: Okay, then let me ask you: If you had to put "69 Restrictions" in a genre, where do you think it would go?

GVC: Ah...

JW: What?

GVC: It's just that, well, "nonfiction" can be interpreted as a pretty broad term. Ditto, "essay," though they're not always necessarily the same thing. Take aphorisms, which are typically accepted as fictions. That is: made-up stories —

JW: Right.

GVC: Right. But many aphorisms *are* essays, regardless, and not in especially zany ways. They proclaim and defend theses, for instance. They follow what Samuel Johnson called a "loose sally of the mind." They journey, they consider, they weigh their own ideas. My point is: I think the essay is more of a mode of writing than a genre, or a form per se. Make it a verb: novels and poems, like nonfiction, can "essay." I think that's what the term "lyric essay" attests to: writing that exists in genre shadowland.

JW: I'm sorry, say that last part again?

GVC: Genre shadowland?

JW: Yes. That makes sense. And as a term, "lyric essay" holds together poetry and nonfiction in a way that I think they're inclined to be. They're much closer together than, say, poetry and fiction because of the intense presence of the self, of the author. Or at the very least, the *site* of the author, if not the author. You know, if you don't want to believe in "the author," which of course, you shouldn't. I guess what the lyric essay does is it allows for the exploration to be seemingly free of the control of the author. Does that sound right?

GVC: It sounds pretty good. So...Aristotle's probable-impossible. Is that the idea that got "69 Restrictions" started?

JW: Well. Sort of. Not really. Actually, I was working in a convenience store, the overnight shift. When I had some time, I'd write. I did two things in the book of poems the "Restrictions" are in. There's another piece called "Things to Do Today." I had this sheet that literally said on it, "Things to Do Today," a big 8½-by-11 sheet of paper with big lines. Just implicitly burdening you with, like, fifty things to do because there were fifty lines. So I started filling it out.

GVC: Because you felt obliged to?

JW: Not obliged exactly. Ultimately a poem feels like a gift. I don't feel like its creator, I feel like its receiver, and my role is a passive one. But of course the poems that people see are ones that I feel work, which is to say, that surprised me and had an effect on me, even though I was the one who wrote it. I guess that's where the difference between a piece of writing being out of your control and only appearing to be. I think lyric essays are much the same.

Aristotle says in the *Poetics* that "the probable impossibility is to be preferred to the improbable possibility." This distinction that he makes is, for me, at the center of everything in this discussion about the line between fiction and nonfiction and poetry and the lyric essay. I don't care what form you write in or how you create. The only thing I care about is whether it works. Whether it fits. The point is whether, when someone reads it, it does something. I mean, did it *surprise* me?

GVC: If a lyric essay's impetus is external, like a poem, where does craft factor in?

JW: The restrictions that are laid out have a narrative arc, of a sort. And I think I was aware of it but I don't think I built it intentionally. I think I intuited it. I think my biggest agency, my biggest decision as far as the will, the autonomy of the will, is where to stop. Because that's to say, "this is its final shape." And, of course, that's why plenty of people want to disregard the idea that anything's ever finished. Sometimes a thing is finished in the sense that it works really well and you're vain enough or appreciative enough to not want to fuck with it anymore. With "69 Restrictions," the culmination rests with the piece's momentum.

GVC: So the finish comes when the idea rolls to a stop?

JW: Yep. That's right.

A HITLER FORGERY"

ON "THE DRY DANUBE: A HITLER FORGERY"

ON "THE DRY DANUBE: A HITLER FORGERY"

ON "THE DRY DANUBE: A HITLER FORGERY"

JOSHUA WHEELER

INTERVIEW WITH PAUL WEST
BY JOSHUA WHEELER

Nothing terrifies like the labyrinths of an evil mind. Paul West's "The Dry Danube: A Hitler Forgery" ushers you into exactly such a place. Were the title simply "Hitler" you might know better than to step inside. That name primes you for hate, makes you dredge up all things monstrous without need for further exploration. But West dangles a lure in the title: "Forgery." He confesses to a ruse straightaway. Have no fear: this monster is not real. You are not asked to suspend disbelief, as with traditional works of fiction, but driven, from the title onward, to acknowledge and investigate your doubt. You commit to what you know is a labyrinth, to what you're told is somehow false, to what you see is uninvitingly dense: 15 pages of unbroken text, block after heavy block, as if the topic, Hitler and the 30 million deaths at his hands, weren't already weighty enough. And then the opening line — "Here I come, slinking brickward in the hour of lavender" — drags you into the essay like a sleazy revision of the final lines of Yeats's "The Second Coming": "And what rough beast, its hour come round at last / Slouches towards Bethlehem to be born?" But this is no birth narrative, no reductive explanation of how Hitler became Hitler.

You begin in a dank doorway across from a classy restaurant in Vienna, in the mind of a struggling young painter observing rich patrons, his thoughts moving through a passionate cycle of grandeur and self-doubt that might characterize any eighteen-year-old art school hopeful. He idealizes and envies his painting mentors, Treischnitt and Kolberhoff, who bombard him with criticism but offer the possibility of a lucrative fellowship. That is the entirety of the plot. You are seduced further and further into the block of text only by the virtuosity of the young man's thoughts, the flow and beauty in his use of language, and the unrelenting conviction that art is his only love. He will suffer in order to preserve beauty for the rest of us. See how he looks upon the women of Vienna:

No man can say he has not come close to losing his divine spark in those eyes, in the fold of flesh they amble about to flaunt, but the most dedicated of us have to keep our mind intact and push our energy into the drab arena of the canvas, the thick paper of ravishing texture.

You know this is foolish and haughty of the young artist, but you also recognize that it is admirable to have such ideals, such commitment to his craft.

He says, "...I am trying to make sense of something that makes none but is merely what happened next. What Happened Next, of which the world is full, poorly as we accommodate ourselves to it." Perhaps this is West's caution that you not read "The Dry Danube" as causal explanation. "What Happened Next" is not a thing that can ever be changed or explained in any satisfactory way; you, reader, are charged with carrying the weight of the incomprehensible horrors of the Holocaust while young Hitler strolls the streets of Vienna with nothing more to do than lament some harsh critiques of his paintings. You might even be excused if you almost forget those horrors because the name "Hitler" appears only in the title. Or you might even be excused if you almost forget those horrors because the voice is capable of such vivid and humorously self-deprecating descriptions, "...there is only that chore in the basement, to which I am bound eventually to be assigned: toilet man, accustomed to the flush and flatus of an entire civilization." Or you might be excused if you almost forget those horrors because West exploits the agility of the essayistic mode to move the young artist from moments of deep introspection to grand, righteous arguments about the unfair expectations and hierarchies of an entrenched artistic tradition: "If I said this out loud, I'd be in real trouble, beating at the bars to get out in time for my nineteenth birthday, one last look at Treischnitt and Kolberhoff, choking on buttercream torte, ever regnant, the semikings, the lickers of all private ice creams."

You might be excused if you find yourself shouting that last part again, "The lickers of all private ice creams!" In that exclamation there is a bit of the playful Wallace Stevens, whose poem "The Emperor of Ice Cream" implores that life is sweet but only while it lasts. The use of "private" makes the exclamation a gorgeously juvenile indictment of the self-important artists who are this young artist's mentors, an irresistible critique of artistic institutions with little notion of flexibility in their form or techniques. The sweetness of life should be available to us all. You cannot help but agree, even if you happen to remember that it is Hitler you are nodding along with.

West has got you trapped in what you know to be the labyrinth of an evil mind, and despite your disgust about all the things that mind is capable of, you are unable to break free from it because you recognize its corridors, because they feel familiar.

But this is no sympathetic portrait of Hitler. West's Hitler is virtuosic and wildly engaging in his idiosyncrasies, but he is also miserably snooty and self-involved. He will repeat countless variations of snoot: "Now they are talking, I imagine, about how, I imagine, I draw. Imagine that." You do not pity this young artist. You do not even necessarily like him, but you see that he is, in all his beautiful and exasperating messiness, undeniably human. And that, you realize, is the real forgery: there is no monster. "The Dry Danube" is an empathetic portrait that demands of you, reader, so much more than the caricatures of Hitler to which you are accustomed. He is not just a reviled patch of hair beneath a nose or a slick comb-over sprouting horns. You do not get to write him off from the start. You cannot use monstrosity as an excuse to resist exploration.

The minotaur in this labyrinth is just a man. And that is maybe the most terrifying revelation — all monsters are us.

West says in his afterword to the novella from which this essay is an excerpt that "the overture to a rampage is perhaps more appalling than the rampage itself." Maybe this is because our histories traditionally strip the rampages down to simple numbers. one regime. six years. thirty million dead. Was the war only six years? Certainly the terror and killing expanded beyond that? Maybe "one regime" is wrong? Was the rampage really just those men, for that short time? The numbers create tidy facts but they dilute all the human messiness, making the terror at once more palatable and totally incomprehensible. Perhaps in the case of "The Dry Danube" the overture is more appalling exactly because we do not have the facts on which to rely. We have only West's imagination. But only in the imagination is there the possibility of empathy, the potential to actually experience the feelings of another. That empathy is what makes delving into the mind of young Hitler so frightening, but it is likely the only antidote for evil — the capacity to feel what your enemy feels. Perhaps all our histories would benefit from a little more of this kind of human messiness, this kind of imagination. Maybe essays born of imagination are exactly where the rehumanization of history is meant to occur.

Joshua Wheeler: You've published thirty novels and twenty books of nonfiction. What do you consider the defining characteristics of each of these genres?

Paul West: Who do you have there who puts me to answer these wonderful questions? Nonfiction is a pretense. Why not do away with it and call the entire expanse of creative writing fiction? All art is created from one person's tangent of reality — birthright, biases, education, the rigmarole that adds up to a life.

JW: So this essay, "The Dry Danube," intends to blur these genre boundaries?

PW: This also applies to the novel I wrote about Hitler and Goebbels, two cross-tempered men with misanthropic versions of the future, both insane and dreaming of a pure future race. Both planned to destroy America. History is always an agreed upon fiction. You ask about "The Dry Danube." I hope it blurs the boundaries to death.

JW: Tell me about the origins of "The Dry Danube."

PW: "Here I come," I introduced myself, with overtures of Rat Man. The author not far behind, anxious not to waste a good idea. I tried, to no end, to write well-behaved historical novels, but to no use. They tended to misbehave from the outset and I ended up committing myself to the wild and woolly, which I adored for its ragamuffin behavior. "The Dry Danube" is as good as you get.

I was roused to greet readers thus, "Here I lurk, a born lurkster," determined to make a mark. There followed Kolberhoff and Treischnitt as followers always do. Whereas my unnamed protagonist rules the roost, given the absolute right to do so. Note how I gave them combined rights to make what they must of the most elegant of fates, beginning their obsequy without ending it.

Who is responsible for "The Dry Danube?" It wrote itself. After the first few words, it flowed and scampered along, berserk as all the best prefer to be. "Big as Portugal," runs one line, and I wish things were so for all of my work; maybe half of it.

I suspect certain readers will say this is a novel out of control, or in the grip of a madman. What is the point of it all? I wish I knew. I kept going from one word to the next because I love writing for its own sake, and devil take the hindmost.

JW: Why not write a more traditional history of Hitler's early years?

PW: Where's the fun in that? Interiority is a superior approach and a far subtler way to render Hitler's tyrannical truth. Try a traditional history for yourself.

JW: But this interiority sings. Why give the maniac such a virtuosic voice?

PW: All of my characters are inflicted with elements of my style — as are the dummies of ventriloquists. I love language too much not to share my word hoard with my characters, even if they are monsters. Hitler and my protagonist overlap time and again, for both have a plenitude of resentment — a human condition which overflows.

I have come to believe in the indestructible resonance of characters' voices — from Nabokov to Henry James to Mary Shelley. And the best of all, Samuel Beckett. You must choose a voice that can insinuate itself through the whole text with it's own soul, of course uttered through the imagination of the novelist. And this duet creates unique insights into human nature. I hope it will always be so — as long as there are books to be read.

JW: And what of the essay's critique of snobbery in the world of high art?

PW: It might be of interest to your readers to know that in this past year I have succumbed to a new passion and had a show of my artwork at the Sola Gallery here in Ithaca. I have dreamed up over one thousand watercolors and collages. Not a bad start. I attribute this success to my mother, a first-rate pianist who also painted, and to my creativity taking a turn toward paint and brush, scissor and glue, instead of the pen. Now I do both, with great joy. I can now relax, no longer disappointing my mother by never learning to play piano.

If I had my time over I might have turned to painting earlier, conscious of a suppressed gift. I should have conquered my dislike of all fruit. Too, I should have conquered my dislike of snow and royalty. Too many aversions, too little sleep.

ABOUT THE COEDITORS

Barret Baumgart received an MFA in Nonfiction from the University of Iowa in 2014. His writing has appeared in *Camera Obscura*, *The Literary Review*, *Seneca Review*, and elsewhere. He currently teaches creative writing courses for the Division of Continuing Education at the University of Iowa.

Suzanne Cody has published essays in anthologies from Seal Press and Random House, and recently produced her first play, a selection of four "performance essays" from her collection *Love. Sex. Shoes*. She is a graduate of the Nonfiction Writing Program at the University of Iowa.

G. V. de Choisy is the nonfiction editor of the *Iowa Review*. Her essays have been published online at *Jezebel*, the *Huffington Post*, and *BuzzFeed*, and will appear in a forthcoming anthology from Atticus Books. She lives in Iowa City, where she hosts *The Lit Show*, a book-talk podcast and radio program.

John D'Agata is the author of *Halls of Fame*, *About a Mountain*, *The Lifespan of a Fact*, and a series of anthologies on the history of the essay, the final installment of which is forthcoming from Graywolf Press. He directs the Nonfiction Writing Program at the University of Iowa.

Lisa Gray Giurato was raised on a farm in rural Iowa and now lives now in Cedar Rapids, Iowa, with her two sons. A graduate of the Nonfiction Writing Program at the University of Iowa, she teaches writing at Coe College, in Iowa.

Michal Milstein is a writer from southern California. The author of *Undisclosed: The Secrets of the AIDS Epidemic from Some Unlikely Sources*, and editor of the journal *Essay Review*, she is a graduate of the Nonfiction Writing Program at the University of Iowa.

Quince Mountain lives in the northwoods of Wisconsin and is currently at work on *You Are a Prince,* a chronicle of belated manhood and unlikely self-help. A graduate of the Nonfiction Writing Program at Iowa, he is an editor of the journal *Killing the Buddha.*

Helen Rubinstein's essays and fiction have appeared in *Ninth Letter, Witness, Slice Magazine, The Best Women's Travel Writing, The New York Times,* and elsewhere. She has an MFA in fiction from Brooklyn College, and currently studies and teaches nonfiction at the University of Iowa's Nonfiction Writing Program.

Joshua Wheeler is a writer from Alamogordo, New Mexico. He has recently published essays in *Harper's, The Sonora Review, Wag's Revue,* and elsewhere. He holds a degree in poetry from the New Mexico State University and is currently a student in the Nonfiction Writing Program at the University of Iowa.

Lawrence Ypil was born in the Philippines and is the recipient of several awards, including a Fulbright Fellowship. The author of *The Highest Hiding Place,* he holds a degree in poetry from Washington University, and is currently studying essays at the University of Iowa's Nonfiction Writing Program.

WE MIGHT AS WELL
CALL IT THE LYRIC ESSAY

WE MIGHT AS WELL
CALL IT THE LYRIC ESSAY

WE MIGHT AS WELL
CALL IT THE LYRIC ESSAY

WE MIGHT AS WELL
CALL IT THE LYRIC ESSAY

WE MIGHT AS WELL

We Might As Well Call It The Lyric Essay:
A Special Issue of *Seneca Review*

Edited by John D'Agata and the graduate students of the Nonfiction Writing
Program at the University of Iowa

Seneca Review: Volume 44/2-45/1
Hobart and William Smith Colleges Press
Geneva, NY 14456

Copyright © 2014 Hobart and William Smith Colleges
ISBN 9781495123948 / ISSN 0037-2145

Printed by Canfield & Tack

Editor, *Seneca Review*: David Weiss

Design: Joshua Unikel

THE ESSAYS

WE MIGHT AS WELL CALL IT
THE LYRIC ESSAY

WE MIGHT AS WELL CALL IT
THE LYRIC ESSAY

WE MIGHT AS WELL CALL IT
THE LYRIC ESSAY

WE MIGHT AS WELL CALL IT
THE LYRIC ESSAY

JOHN D'AGATA

We might as well call it the lyric essay because I don't think "essay" means for most readers what essayists hope it does.

Or, we might as well call it the lyric essay because "nonfiction" is far too limiting.

Or, we might as well call it the lyric essay because "creative nonfiction" — let's face it — is desperate.

Then again, as literary terms go, "lyric essay" is no less an example of lipstick on a pig — which I think is why you'll find that it has fallen out of favor with a lot of the writers in this book.

It has fallen out with us as well, its editors.

And yet, fifteen years ago, when I was a student in a nonfiction writing program, the term felt like an extraordinary gift. I was in grad school during the late 1990s, and at that time it seemed that memoir was all that anyone was talking about. I wasn't writing memoir, however, and because I was young and naive and phenomenally self-involved, I started to believe that I had made a mistake, that nonfiction was not the genre for me, that I didn't have a literary home. I joined our university's neighboring poetry program, yet because I insisted on submitting 20-page-long essays to my poetry workshops, it was clear that that genre was not going to be home either.

Nevertheless, I liked the challenge of writing in-between the two worlds of poetry and essay, and as these things go when you're fully immersed in a new and exciting passion, I started to see everything through the lens of that hybridity.

Anne Carson came to our program with her first American book, and I swear I heard her use the words "lyric" and "essay" in close proximity to one another, describing what she liked about some ancient Greek writer. Then Michael Ondaantje visited soon after, and he used the term "lyrical nonfiction" to describe what he liked about Carson. In class, one of my favorite professors often casually referred to "lyric forms of the essay," as if it were a loosely held secret that we were being let in on, like

directions to the world's swankiest bar that had no signage and only a back door. And then one day over email, my old college mentor, Deborah Tall, told me that the frustrations with genre that I was experiencing at the moment were not particularly new. She pointed me in the direction of a dozen or so texts from antiquity, the middle ages, and contemporary Europe that all toyed formally with lines between poetry and essays. "Check out these 'lyric essays,'" she wrote.

And soon enough, the term seemed to appear everywhere thereafter. Tom Simmons, our graduate school professor, offered a course on the lyric essay. *The New Yorker* referred to some new book as a series of lyric essays. And many of us started submitting new work in our classes with the willfully forceful subtitle *A lyric essay*.

Initially I liked the term merely for how it sounded, and then for its slight implication of literary nonsense, and later for how it seemed to eschew the story-driven ambitions of fiction and nonfiction for the associative inquiry of poems.

Eventually, I was sold. And within a year of first hearing the term I started editing a section of *Seneca Review* that was devoted to lyric essays. Fifteen years later, I am still editing that section.

During the intervening years, however, I've moved away from using the term myself. These days I don't refer to what I like to read or write as "lyric essays," even though I still read a lot of the same stuff. I don't teach the term often either, and hardly use it in criticism. It's not that I've stopped finding the term interesting or useful; instead, as I got older and started to explore the history of the good old-fashioned essay, I began to find that everything that I loved about "lyric essays" was already represented in much of the essay's past. What I therefore hoped, or what I naively assumed, was that if we could remind ourselves as essayists of the variety of essays that have been written in our genre, we'd have no need for terms that try to stake their claim on narrowly conceived interpretations of the genre.

But then something changed my mind. I wrote a book, *The Lifespan of a Fact*, that proved to be controversial. It upset people because it suggested that some kinds of essays don't always need to be verifiably accurate, that we can appreciate some essays for the experiences they are sharing, and the emotions that they are conjuring, rather than the facts or information they relay. I was shocked by some people's reactions, however. I was expecting some kick-back from journalists, who huddle with us beneath that big umbrella term of "nonfiction," but who clearly are

engaged in a sacred social service whose stakes are considerably higher, more timely, and thus more consequential — socially speaking, I mean — than the stylized recollections that we share in our memoirs.

Except, according to many other nonfiction writers, that "sacred social service" that journalists are engaged in also apparently applies to memoirs — and to travelogues, meditations, portraits, etc. If it's called "nonfiction," many colleagues insisted, then it needs to report the facts as accurately as the news.

One famous writer went as far to say in a tweet that if a nonfiction text does not adhere to the rules of journalism then that text is nothing but a "hoax" — thus swiftly rendering everything that's huddled under that big umbrella term of "nonfiction" as either 100 percent verifiable . . . or not nonfiction at all.

And that's what was most disturbing. Because what I love to read in nonfiction often exists between those poles of what's verifiable and what's simply not. I love the in-between, which is where I think the most truthful struggles with reality exist. The history of our genre attests to this, rich as it is with woefully unverifiable essays by Virginia Woolf, Plutarch, George Orwell, Herodotus, E. B. White, Cicero, Joseph Mitchell, Daniel Defoe, Jorge Louis Borges, James Thurber, Natalia Ginzburg, Truman Capote, W. G. Sebald, Mary McCarthy, Sei Shonagon, and many, many others.

I don't want to lose them, cast them out of this genre. And neither do I think we can afford to lose whatever writers are yet to emerge in our genre who might be inspired by those nonfiction forebears who have interpreted the rules differently. After all, is there any single term that could possibly describe how we each process the world?

In some ways, twenty-five hundred years ago, Plato asked the same. In *Symposium*, he tells us a relatively simple story about some friends at a dinner party who talk about love. Surrounding Plato's story about that party, however, is the philosopher's own story about how he heard the story.

According to Plato, a man named Aristodemus, who had attended the dinner party, told his friends Apollodorus and Phoinix about the conversation that evening. Phoinix then told his friend about the party, and that friend told it to Glaucon, and then Glaucon told it to Plato. But Glaucon isn't sure that he remembers the story correctly, so he looks to Apollodorus to clarify some details, even though Apollodorus wasn't actually at the party, but instead had only heard about it from Aristodemus,

who was.

Why is this important? At first it's hard to say why any of it is important, and so we temporarily forget about these elaborate machinations once Plato starts telling us about the party itself. What we learn is that several people made speeches at the party, and all of them had opinions about the meaning of love. Socrates too was at this dinner party, and when he finally speaks up he tells his dinner companions about a woman named Diotima, a priestess whom he knew while growing up in Athens and who had once shared with Socrates her own thoughts about love.

When we're young, she said, we begin by loving a body, and then we learn eventually how to love different bodies, and then how to love souls, and then customs, and then finally knowledge.

Love, it turns out, is multilayered, like most things. But by the time we learn this in Plato's *Symposium*, we're hearing it from a fifth-hand source, so the story is a little fuzzy. On top of this, the story comes from a party that took place back when Socrates was still alive — fifteen years earlier than when Plato is writing *Symposium* — and the crux of Plato's essay isn't even that story about the party itself, but the story that's told by Socrates at the party about his youth — a story within a story within an essay, it turns out — remembered from a moment in Socrates's life that happened sixty years earlier than when he shares it with his friends. So seventy-five years and six retellings later, what we learn in the *Symposium* is that knowledge is layered, too. It's complicated, multidimensional, unpredictable, very messy, and we probably couldn't agree on what it really is or how it's ever made or the best way it to frame it for someone else to appreciate.

And this is why the *Symposium* is itself so very messy, multidimensional, multilayered, and difficult to interpret with any kind of confidence. Knowledge, real knowledge, is problematic the moment we start trying to nail it down.

The lesson here, to my ear at least, is wonderfully applicable to the nonfiction world. If Plato were with us now, I'd like to imagine him intervening in the hothouse debates that fester in our genre, casting a simple question into the fever swamps of the internet: Do we really all believe there's only one way to make an essay?

Despite its clumsy title, then, this is not an anthology about the dangers or virtues of "nonfiction," "creative nonfiction," "flash" this, "long form" that, or any other terms we might throw against the genre in hopes of finding something that might finally stick. This is an anthology about the beautiful gangly breadth

of this unnameable literary form, and how nomenclature, while often limiting, polarizing, inadequate, and always stupid, can also be the thing that opens up our genre to new possibilities and new paths of inquiry, helping us to shape our experiences in the world in ways we have not yet imagined. We might as well call it the lyric essay, therefore, because we need as many terms as there are passions for this form.

THE PAIN SCALE

THE PAIN SCALE

THE PAIN SCALE

THE PAIN SCALE

EULA BISS

SPRING 2005

0 $\longrightarrow$

No Pain

The concept of Christ is considerably older than the concept of zero. Both are problematic — both have their fallacies and their immaculate conceptions. But the problem of zero troubles me significantly more than the problem of Christ.

I am sitting in the exam room of a hospital entertaining the idea that absolutely no pain is not possible. Despite the commercials, I suspect that pain cannot be eliminated. And this may be the fallacy on which we have based all our calculations and all our excesses. All our sins are for zero.

Zero is not a number. Or at least, it does not behave like a number. It does not add, subtract, or multiply like other numbers. Zero is a number in the way that Christ was a man.

Aristotle, for one, did not believe in zero.

If no pain is possible, then, another question — is no pain desirable? Might the absence of pain equal the absence of everything?

Some very complicated mathematical problems cannot be solved without the concept of zero. But zero makes some very simple problems impossible to solve. For example, the value of zero divided by zero is unknown.

I am not a mathematician. I am sitting in a hospital trying to measure my pain on a scale from zero to ten. For this purpose, I need a zero. A scale of any sort needs fixed points.

The upper fixed point on the Fahrenheit scale, ninety-six, is based on a slightly inaccurate measure of normal body temperature. The lower fixed point, zero, is the coldest temperature at which a mixture of salt and water can still remain liquid. I myself am a mixture of salt and water. I strive to remain liquid.

Zero, on the Celsius scale, is the point at which water freezes. And one hundred is the point at which water boils. But Anders Celsius, who introduced the scale in 1741, originally fixed zero as the point at which water boils, and one hundred as the point at which water freezes. These fixed points were reversed only after his death.

The deepest circle of Dante's *Inferno* does not burn. It is frozen. In his last glimpse of Hell, Dante looks back and sees Satan upside down through the ice.

There is only one fixed point on the Kelvin scale — absolute zero. Absolute zero is 273 degrees Celsius colder than the temperature at which water freezes. There are zeroes beneath zeroes. Absolute zero is the temperature at which molecules and atoms are moving as slowly as possible. But even at absolute zero, their motion does not stop completely. Even the absolute is not absolute. This is comforting, but it does not give me faith in zero.

At night, I ice my pain. My mind descends into a strange sinking calm. Any number multiplied by zero is zero. And so with ice and me. I am nullified. I wake up to melted ice and the warm throb of my pain returning.

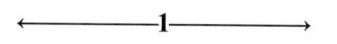

Where does pain worth measuring begin? With a hang nail? With a stubbed toe? A sore throat? A needle prick? A razor cut?

My father is a physician. He treats patients with cancer, who often suffer extreme pain. My father raised me to believe that most pain is minor. He was never impressed by my bleeding cuts or even my weeping sores. In retrospect, neither am I.

My father once told me that an itch is just very mild pain. Both sensations simply signal, he told me, irritated or damaged tissue.

But a nasty itch, I have observed, can be much more excruciating than a paper cut, which is also mild pain. Digging at an itch until it bleeds and is transformed into pure pain can bring a kind of relief.

When I complained of pain as a child, my father would ask, "What kind of pain?" Wearily, he would list for me some of the different kinds of pain, "Burning, stabbing, throbbing, prickling, dull, sharp, deep, shallow...."

Hospice nurses are trained to identify five types of pain: physical, emotional, spiritual, social, and financial.

The pain of feeling, the pain of caring, the pain of doubting, the pain of parting, the pain of paying.

But then there is also the pain of longing, the pain of desire, the pain of sore muscles, which I find pleasurable....

The pain of learning, and the pain of reading.

The pain of trying.

The pain of living.

There is a mathematical proof that zero equals one. Which, of course, it doesn't.

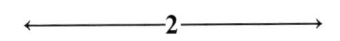

The set of whole numbers is also known as "God's numbers."

The devil is in the fractions.

Although the distance between one and two is finite, it contains infinite fractions. This could also be said of the distance between my mind and my body. My one and my two. My whole and its parts.

The sensations of my own body may be the only subject on which I am qualified to claim expertise. Sad and terrible, then, how

little I know. "How do you feel?" the doctor asks, and I cannot answer. Not accurately. "Does this hurt?" he asks. Again, I'm not sure. "Do you have more or less pain than the last time I saw you?" Hard to say. I begin to lie to protect my reputation. I try to act certain.

The physical therapist raises my arm above my head. "Any pain with this?" she asks. Does she mean any pain in addition to the pain I already feel, or does she mean any pain at all? She is annoyed by my question. "Does this cause you pain?" she asks curtly. No. She bends my neck forward, "Any pain with this?" No. "Any pain with this?" No. It feels like a lie every time.

On occasion, an extraordinary pain swells like a wave under the hands of the doctor, or the chiropractor, or the massage therapist, and floods my body. Sometimes I hear my throat make a sound. Sometimes I see spots. I consider this the pain of treatment, and I have come to find it deeply pleasurable. I long for it.

The International Association for the Study of Pain is very clear on this point — pain must be unpleasant. "Experiences which resemble pain but are not unpleasant," reads their definition of pain, "should not be called pain."

In the second circle of Dante's *Inferno*, the adulterous lovers cling to each other, whirling eternally, caught in an endless wind. My next-door neighbor, who loves Chagall, does not think this sounds like Hell. I think it depends on the wind.

Wind, like pain, is difficult to capture. The poor wind-sock is always striving, and always falling short.

It took sailors more than two hundred years to develop a standardized numerical scale for the measure of wind. The result, the Beaufort scale, provides twelve categories for everything from "Calm" to "Hurricane." The scale offers not just a number, but a term for the wind, a range of speed, and a brief description.

A force 2 wind on the Beaufort scale, for example, is a "Light Breeze" moving between four and seven miles per hour. On land, it is specified as "wind felt on face; leaves rustle; ordinary vanes moved by wind."

Left alone in the exam room I stare at the pain scale, a simple number line complicated by only two phrases. Under zero: "no pain." Under ten: "the worst pain imaginable."

The worst pain imaginable . . . . Skinned alive? Impaled with hundreds of nails? Dragged over gravel behind a fast truck?

Determining the intensity of my own pain is a blind calculation. On my first attempt, I assigned the value of ten to a theoretical experience — burning alive. Then I tried to determine what percentage of the pain of burning alive I was feeling.

I chose 30 percent — three. Which seemed, at the time, quite substantial.

Three. Mail remains unopened. Thoughts are rarely followed to their conclusions. Sitting still becomes unbearable after one hour. Nausea sets in. Quiet desperation descends.

"Three is nothing," my father tells me now. "Three is go home and take two aspirin."

It would be helpful, I tell him, if that could be noted on the scale.

The four vital signs used to determine the health of a patient are blood pressure, temperature, breath, and pulse. Recently, it has been suggested that pain be considered a fifth vital sign. But pain presents a unique problem in terms of measurement, and a unique cruelty in terms of suffering — it is entirely subjective.

Assigning a value to my own pain has never ceased to feel like a political act. I am a citizen of a country that ranks our comfort above any other concern. People suffer, I know, so that I may eat bananas in February. And then there is history . . . . I struggle to consider my pain in proportion to the pain of a napalmed Vietnamese girl whose skin is slowly melting off as she walks naked in the sun. This exercise itself is painful.

"You are not meant to be rating world suffering," my friend in Honduras advises. "This scale applies only to you and your

experience."

At first, this thought is tremendously relieving. It unburdens me of factoring the continent of Africa into my calculations. But I hate the knowledge that I am isolated in this skin — alone with my pain and my own fallibility.

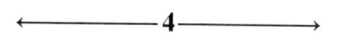

The Wong-Baker Faces Scale was developed to help young children rate their pain. It features a smiley face at zero "No Hurt" and a crying face at five "Hurts Worst." In between are a nervous smile, a straight-mouthed stare, a slight grimace, and a deep frown.

The face I remember as the face of pain was on the front page of a local newspaper in an Arizona gas station. The man's face was horrifyingly distorted in an open-mouthed cry. His house, the caption explained, had just been destroyed in a wildfire. But the man himself, the article revealed, had not been hurt.

Several studies have suggested that children using the Wong-Baker Scale tend to conflate emotional pain and physical pain. A child who is not in physical pain but is very frightened of surgery, for example, might choose the crying face. One researcher observed that "hurting" and "feeling" seemed to be synonymous to some children. I myself am puzzled by the distinction at times. After all, pain is defined as a "sensory and emotional experience." In an attempt to rate only the physical pain of children, a more emotionally "neutral" scale was developed. The faces on this scale appear alien, and the first four nearly indistinguishable expressions of neutrality followed by a wince and then an open-mouthed shout.

A group of adult patients favored the Wong-Baker Scale in a study comparing several different types of pain scales. The patients were asked to identify the easiest scale to use by rating all the scales on a scale from zero: "not easy" to six: "easiest ever seen." The patients were then asked to rate how well the scales represented pain on a scale from zero: "not good" to six: "best ever seen." The patients were not invited to rate the experience of rating.

I stare at a newspaper photo of an Israeli boy with a bloodstained cloth wrapped around his forehead. His face is impassive.

I stare at a newspaper photo of an Iraqi prisoner standing delicately balanced with electrodes attached to his body, his head covered with a hood.

No face, no pain?

A crying baby has always seemed to me to be in the worst pain imaginable. But when my aunt became a nurse twenty-five years ago, it was not unusual for surgery to be done on infants without any pain medication. Babies, it was believed, did not have the fully developed nervous systems necessary to feel pain. Medical evidence that infants experience pain in response to anything that would cause an adult pain has only recently emerged.

There is no evidence of pain on my body. No marks. No swelling. No terrible tumor. The X-Rays revealed nothing. Two MRIs of my brain and spine revealed nothing. Nothing was infected and festering, as I had suspected and feared. There was no ghastly huge white cloud on the film. There was nothing to illustrate my pain except a number, which I was told to choose from between zero and ten. My proof.

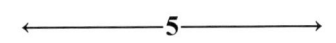

"The problem with scales from zero to ten," my father tells me, "is the tyranny of the mean."

Overwhelmingly, patients tend to rate their pain as a five, unless they are in excruciating pain. At best, this renders the scale far less sensitive to gradations in pain. At worst, it renders the scale useless.

I understand the desire to be average only when I am in pain. To be normal is to be okay in a fundamental way — to be chosen numerically by God.

When I could no longer sleep at night because of my pain, my father reminded me that a great many people suffer from both

insomnia and pain. "In fact," he told me, "neck and back pain is so common that it is a cliché — a pain in the neck!"

The fact that 50 million Americans suffer from chronic pain does not comfort me. Rather, it confounds me. "This is not normal," I keep thinking. A thought invariably followed by a doubt, "Is this normal?"

The distinction between test results that are normal or abnormal is often determined by how far the results deviate from the mean. My X-rays did not reveal a cause for my pain, but they did reveal an abnormality. "See this," the doctor pointed to the string of vertebrae hanging down from the base of my skull like a loose line finding plumb. "Your spine," he told me, "is abnormally straight."

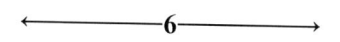

A force 6 wind on the Beaufort scale, a "Strong Breeze," is characterized by "large branches in motion; telegraph wires whistle; umbrellas used with difficulty."

Over a century before preliminary scales were developed to quantify the wind, serious efforts were made to produce an accurate map of Hell. Infernal cartography was considered an important undertaking for the architects and mathematicians of the Renaissance, who based their calculations on the distances and proportions described by Dante. The exact depth and circumference of Hell inspired intense debates, despite the fact that all calculations, no matter how sophisticated, were based on a work of fiction.

Galileo Galilei delivered extensive lectures on the mapping of Hell. He applied recent advances in geometry to determine the exact location of the entrance to the underworld and then figured the dimensions that would be necessary to maintain the structural integrity of Hell's interior.

It was the age of the golden rectangle — the divine proportion. Mathematics revealed God's plan. But the very use of numbers required a religious faith, because one could drop off the edge of the earth at any point. The boundaries of the maps at that time

faded into oceans full of monsters.

Imagination is treacherous. It erases distant continents, it builds a Hell so real that the ceiling is vulnerable to collapse.

To be safe, I think I should map my pain only in proportion to pain I have already felt. But my nerves have short memories. My mind remembers crashing my bicycle as a teenager, but my body does not. I cannot seem to conjure the sensation of lost skin without actually losing skin. My nerves cannot, or will not, imagine past pain — and this, I think, is for the best. Nerves simply register, they do not invent.

But after a year of pain, I realized that I could no longer remember what it felt like not to be in pain. I was left anchorless. For a while, I tended to think of the time before the pain as easier and brighter, but then I began to suspect myself of fantasy and nostalgia.

Eventually, I discovered that with some effort I could imagine the sensation of pain as heat, which brought a kind of relief.

Perhaps, with a stronger mind, I could imagine the heat as warmth, and then the warmth as nothing at all.

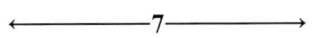

I accidentally left a burner on the stove going for two and a half days — a small blue flame, burning and burning . . . . The duration terrified me. How incredibly dangerous, so many hours of fire.

When I cry from the pain, I cry over the idea of it lasting forever, not over the pain itself. The psychologist, in her rational way, suggests that I do not let myself imagine it lasting forever. "Choose an amount of time that you know you can endure," she suggests, "and then challenge yourself only to make it through that time." I make it through the night, and then sob through half the morning.

The pain scale measures only the intensity of pain, not the duration. This may be its greatest flaw. A measure of pain, I

believe, requires at least two dimensions. The suffering of Hell is terrifying not because of any specific torture, but because it is eternal.

The square root of seven results in a decimal that repeats randomly into infinity. The exact figure cannot be known, only a close approximation. Rounding a number to the nearest significant figure is a tool designed for the purpose of making measurements. The practicality of rounding is something my mind can fully embrace. No measurement is ever exact, of course.

Seven is the largest prime number between zero and ten. Out of all the numbers, the very largest primes are unknown. Still, every year, the largest known prime is larger. Euclid proved the number of primes to be infinite, but the infinity of primes may be slightly smaller than the infinity of the rest of the numbers. It is here, exactly at this point, that my ability to comprehend begins to fail.

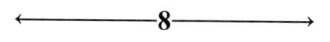

Although all the numbers follow each other in a predictable line, many unknown quantities exist.

Experts do not know why some pain resolves and other pain becomes chronic. One theory is that the body begins to react to its own reaction, trapping itself in a cycle of its own pain response. This can go on indefinitely, twisting like the figure eight of infinity.

My father tells me that when he broke his collarbone it didn't hurt. I would like to believe this, but I am suspicious of my father's assessment of his own pain.

The problem with pain is that I cannot feel my father's, and he cannot feel mine. This, I suppose, is also the essential mercy of pain.

Several recent studies have suggested that women feel pain differently than men. Further studies have suggested that pain medications act differently on women than they do on men. I am suspicious of these studies, so favored by *Newsweek*, and so heaped

upon waiting room tables. I dislike the idea that our flesh is so essentially unique that it does not even register pain as a man's flesh does — a fact that renders our bodies, again, objects of supreme mystery.

But I am comforted, oddly, by the possibility that you cannot compare my pain to yours. And, for that reason, cannot prove it insignificant.

The medical definition of pain specifies the "presence or potential of tissue damage." Pain that does not signal tissue damage is not, technically, pain.

"This is a pathology," the doctor assured me when he informed me that there was no definitive cause of my pain, no effective treatment for it, and very probably no end to it. "This is not in your head."

It would not have occurred to me to think that I was imagining the pain. But the longer the pain persisted, and the harder it became for me to imagine what it was like not to be in pain, the more seriously I considered the disturbing possibility that perhaps I was not, in fact, in pain.

Another theory of chronic pain is that it is a faulty message sent by malfunctioning nerves. "For example," the Mayo Clinic suggests, "your pain could be similar to the phantom pain some amputees feel in their amputated limbs."

I walked out of a lecture on chronic pain after too many repetitions of the phrase, "We have reason to believe that you are in pain, even if there is no physical evidence of your pain." I had not realized that the fact that I believed myself to be in pain was not reason enough.

We have reason to believe in infinity, but everything we know ends.

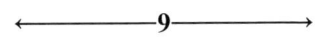

"I breathe, I have a heartbeat, I have pain..." I repeat to myself as I lie in bed at night. I am striving to adopt the pain as a vital

sensation.

Once, for a study of chronic pain, I was asked to rate not just my pain, but also my suffering. I rated my pain as a three. Having been sleepless for nearly a week, I rated my suffering as a seven.

"Pain is the hurt, either physical or emotional, that we experience," writes the Reverend James Chase. "Suffering is the story we tell ourselves of our pain."

Yes, suffering is the story we tell ourselves.

"If we come to the point where we have no place for suffering," Reverend Chase writes, "to what lengths will we go to eradicate it? Will we go so far as to inflict suffering to end it?"

Christianity is not mine. I do not know it and I cannot claim it. But I have seen the sacred heart ringed with thorns, the gaping wound in Christ's side, the weeping virgin, the blood, the nails, the cross to bear . . . . Pain is holy, I understand. Suffering is divine.

In my worst pain, I can remember thinking, "This is not beautiful." I can remember being disgusted by the very idea.

But in my worst pain, I also found myself secretly cherishing the phrase, "This too shall pass." The longer the pain lasted, the more beautiful and impossible and absolutely holy this phrase became.

←————————10
The Worst Pain Imaginable

Through a failure of my imagination, or of myself, I have discovered that the pain I am in is always the worst pain imaginable.

But I would like to believe that there is an upper limit to pain. That there is a maximum intensity nerves can register.

There is no tenth circle to Dante's Hell.

23

The digit ten depends on the digit zero in our current number system. In 1994 an Alternative Number System was developed. "This system," its creator wrote with triumph, "eliminates the need for the digit zero, and hence all digits behave the same."

"One of the functions of the pain scale," my father explains, "is to protect doctors — to spare them some emotional pain. Hearing someone describe their pain as a ten is much easier than hearing them describe it as a hot poker driven through their eyeball into their brain."

A better scale, my father thinks, might rate what patients would be willing to do to relieve their pain. "Would you," he suggests, "visit five specialists and take three prescription narcotics?" I laugh because I have done just that. "Would you," I offer, "give up a limb?" I would not. "Would you surrender your sense of sight for the next ten years?" my father asks. I would not. "Would you accept a shorter life span?" I might. We are laughing, having fun with this game. But later, reading statements collected by the American Pain Foundation, I am alarmed by the number of references to suicide.

The description of hurricane force winds on the Beaufort scale is simply, "devastation occurs."

Bringing us, of course, back to zero.

TOO MANY SPIRITS WHO
BEGGED TO BE LET IN

TOO MANY SPIRITS WHO
BEGGED TO BE LET IN

TOO MANY SPIRITS WHO
BEGGED TO BE LET IN

TOO MANY SPIRITS WHO
BEGGED TO BE LET IN

JENNY BOULLY

FALL 2007

When the girl was returned — it was discovered that she had been gutted, and her cavity was filled with paper money. There was 3,000 baht. Her grandmother was the woman with no teeth. That's what I called her. I would tell my mother, I'm going to go buy a soda from the woman with no teeth. Tell your mother, the woman with no teeth would say, tell your mother that today we have corn.

Some things happen from the inside out: existence, for instance; or, forming into a little body then being born; or, the intense compression of matter before the Big Bang then the expansion of the universe; or, the intense compression of thought before the expansion of the essay. Some things happen from the inside out: love, for instance; or, the holding in of something for a very long time before letting it live outside of you; writing, for instance.

My cousin grows mushrooms. They creep out at night from plastic balloons that line a dark and dank hut. The oyster mushrooms are my favorite — they're fleshy and gray and smooth; they fan out like something yearning. He makes fresh curry and steams the oyster mushrooms in a banana leaf for me. He sells what we don't eat.

In the early morning, my aunt goes into the forest to rummage for wild mushrooms. I point to one and ask if we can eat it. That one, she says, is a *kee-kwai* mushroom, or, a mushroom that rises from the shit of a cow or water buffalo. When she was a child, she and my mother would forage every morning for mushrooms. They would sell what they could not, what they wanted to eat.

Somewhere, in another world, the essay wants to tell you that there is nothing. There is only whiteness, a white swallow, a few semicolons, a parenthesis. I can't think of *only nothing*. My mind wants to think in terms of white: white curtains, white bedding,

a white wedding dress, a white handkerchief, a blank sheet of white paper, a dizzy, smoky memory, a few stars shimmering, snow on the TV, a white dusting covering everything.

I feel as if I should share with you the exact circumstances — the time, the people, the place, but the essay doesn't reserve a space for these. Instead, I see a crematorium. It's white. It's at the temple. The monks will handle the girl's body from here on and then something else will help it come out of this world and into the next. Some things start from the inside out; dying, for instance. Someone shoots a canon, or what to me sounds like a canon. My mother tells me that the canon is meant to signal to the little girl where her spirit is to go.

The village doctor told her that she was sick, really sick, that she needed to go to the hospital. There, the doctor told her that she was fine, to go home. No, the village doctor said, you need to go into town, to the hospital there. The village hospital kept saying that she was fine, to go home. She died three days later. She was four. At the funeral, a neighbor retold this story. The doctor, the one that kept sending her home, was playing with his cell phone.

The crematorium smoke rises white into the air, then gray, then black. There is a procession of fireworks, the kind that just make a lot of noise without producing light. It's a scary place, the crematorium; only monks are allowed to see what goes on in there.

Because some things on the outside want to work their way back into the inside: a small village in Korat, Thailand, last summer, my mother, my sisters, and me.

My mother told me that when she was young, she carried wares through the cemetery, and she could hear the juices of the rotting bodies dripping; she could not run, although she was so scared; she could not risk spilling the food she had so carefully prepared to sell. Some days, she would go about the market and collect rice that others had spilled; some days, she would only gather about half a cup.

When I went to visit for the first time, my ancestors tried to keep me in the country of my birth. They did not like that one of their own had gone to the outside, to the country outside. They did not like that my father had come from the outside and taken

some of their own to this outside country. My mother knew that they would want to touch my sisters and me; she prayed that they might look but not touch. All night, my sisters and I had bad dreams, and we could see them, with their yellow eyes, yellow skin, yellow teeth, yellow fingernails, looking. I am sick for a day before I do as my mom says, to pray to something big that I do not know. My little sister, being so young and defenseless, suffered fever for four days. When I describe the beings in my dreams, my mother says that they are dead family, knows which ghost is great grandfather. She says that tomorrow, when we go to visit Johor, a town whose name is contained in our family name, there will be more ghosts. My cousin gives me a Buddha charm on a piece of holy string to wear, tells me how to pray and *wai* before letting it fall over my head.

The little girl died, the villagers said, because she had a hole in her lung. The little girl was my cousin, once removed. The people who live in her house, the house she wants to get back into, lay still at night. They are afraid of the four-year-old girl. The little girl's mother went away one day; she said that she was going to work in Bangkok; she said that she was only going for two weeks; she never came back, and the little girl never saw her again. The little girl's father got a new wife and ignored the little girl. Somehow she began to live with the people next door. She learned to call the lady in that house mother.

One day, some friends take us on a tour of the fruit farms of Korat. We visit a vineyard where the grapes will be made into wine. Korat, because it is mountainous, does have a chill in the air everyday, isn't as hot as the rest of the country. I guess that is why there are vineyards here. Our friend asks us to taste the grapes; he says that they are sweet. He even makes a face that indicates that the grape is too sweet. To me, the grapes aren't sweet at all. I tell myself that it's because the grapes in America are probably manufactured to be supersweet, that my palate can only register sweet at those levels.

Then we visit a place that isn't a fruit farm at all; it's a flower farm, but there is only one type of flower. It's a funeral flower. These are flowers for those who have already died, our friend says. He asks the attendant to cut some for us.

Once, my mother was so sick that disemboweled ghosts came to visit her all day and all night. They were child ghosts; they

begged her to go play outside. They said that it was fun, that they had food for her. My mother, sick and hungry, went to play with them in the forests; she did not, however, eat their food. The next day, she was almost dead.

(I need to finish this essay soon — the ghosts are coming to visit me. I hear floorboards creaking in places where they should not creak. Someone is walking about. It always happens this way — the Thai dead, my family, do not like for me to write about them. Tonight, like always when I write about them, they will visit me in dreams. They will give me fever. They will try to take me away so that I can't write about them anymore. It's morning; I am alone and have no Buddha statues here. I should have listened to my mother when she said, here, take this with you to keep away your bad dreams.)

Next time you come here, all these children will have children of their own, my mother says to me.

The flowers are white anthirriums. They don't even look real. They look fake, something manufactured by man. They live longer than our cut orchids; they live longer than the other vased flowers; when they finally do begin to die, they shake black ash on themselves out of their stamens. Their flesh begins to curl, begins to blacken. I ask our nephew to take the flowers outside, to burn them with the garbage.

It might appear that this one house is having a celebration, that they are so happy that the little girl is dead, and that's why they are playing their music so loudly. It might appear this way, but I know better. This one house is not playing happy songs. I know these songs; they are the old folk songs of Korat, stories about the poor, the hungry, the hard working. These songs say they glimpse something worth living for; these songs say *someday* and *if only*.

Once, in a tourism guidebook for Thailand, I read that visitors should steer clear of Korat, that there simply isn't anything there, that the people there live as they've lived, in disgusting squalor, for hundreds of years, that there simply isn't anything *to do* there.

One year, I was too scared to go to Thailand. Sometime, in the middle of the night, my uncle and aunt and cousin were shot in the

head, execution style. My mother said that nothing could be done.

She was in the cornfield with her granddaughter; they were pulling off the ears; they would make five baht for each kilo bag. A van pulled up to the cornfield; a masked man grabbed the girl; the woman with no teeth wouldn't let go. The man cut the girl's arm off with a knife; the woman with no teeth.

(The essay doesn't want to break apart, does not want to scatter itself, and, like its writer, wants to live forever.)

My mother's mother, seeing how sick her daughter was, scooped her into a basket that yoked about her neck and wandered the countryside, looking for a monk to help her. There was no money for a doctor. In the other basket, my grandmother carried some rice. They eventually met a monk who chanted over my mother, touched her, blessed her, read her future. She will not die, he said, but she will grow to have enormous wings and fly far, far away from you. But she will be back; she will fly back and forth, back and forth the whole of her life.

The dead want to go *inside*; they want to live inside the houses where the living live. When you build your house in Thailand, you must have the monks come and perform your housewarming blessing; otherwise, the spirits of the land, the spirits of all of those who have lived on this land before you, will come in and take their place among you. The monks will chant, will try to placate them, will try to help the dead understand that the living must be here now, that they must instead reside inside the little spirit house that has been put there on the land for them. You see, the monks say, there are even little ladders there to help you climb up, to help you get *in*.

One summer, we kept hearing the ghost of a little boy. He begged to come inside. He walked around and around our house all night; in the morning, we could see a worn path around the house's perimeter; each day, this path got deeper and wider. We bought more and more gifts to the spirit houses on the property, but the little boy kept crying, saying that he wanted to be let in.

For the Thai people, there are only two places you could possibly live: *mueng Thai* and *mueng nogk*. *Mueng nogk* means "the country outside" or "the outside country" or simply, any country outside

of the country of Thailand. If you are not *in here*, then you are *outside*, and your little spirit begs and begs to be let in again.

Before her father died, my mother was allowed to go to school. After that, she was made to work in rice fields. She was six years old. Then, her mother sent her away to work in someone's house and rice fields. My grandmother showed up once a week for payment, and once a month, she got bags of rice. When she was twelve, my mother ran away. She continued to work in people's houses; she continued to labor in fields. I liked school, she said.

The music goes on for days, but it stops once. The monks have come to chant; they will stay the night with the family of that house. They will sprinkle the doorways and the windows with holy water to keep the spirit of the little girl out; the men of that one house have all shaved their heads, have gone to the temple to become monks so that they can help the little girl go to heaven.

Thailand is full of ghosts. I believe in ghosts there, but not so much here. Heraclitus said that in the afterlife, souls communicate through the sense of smell. Thailand smells like too much life — too much rain, too many trees, an abundance of fruit and geckos, red earth, tamarind trees. Some mornings, it wasn't the smell of flowers or just-cooked rice, but rather the smell of dark, of dankness, of my cousin's mushrooms creeping, of something urging to come in between. It is something black and nebulous; I scare myself when I dream in dark hues — midnight blue, crimson red, rust, forest green.

Perhaps they were using the girl for body parts — kidneys, her liver, her heart. But there are other little girls too, my mother tells me, not just the granddaughter of the woman with no teeth. Maybe there is a sick sexual maniac who likes young girls and then wants to kill them afterward, I say. Do they just cut into the girls, or do they give them something to ease the pain? It must hurt so much, my mother says, especially if you're a young girl.

When the author wants to keep going, when the author wants something to click, to take hold, the essay begs to be broken apart. (I thought I should take the last paragraph, the one above this one, and cut it in half or tear it in half and then cut and paste it here below this one, but that thought was in the early stages of my thinking about this essay. It was something that I was

excited about, that I felt strongly about. I thought I would have a lot of visuals to give you, but that was before I began to write, before the inside began to live on the outside. In essay writing, sometimes, the impetus is not carried out in the execution.)

I wanted to supply a world without pretext, have the action occur right away. Rather than fill in the details, I would prefer to talk about something else here, hope that, in the end, it will all come together again, that it will all somehow make sense. Some things begin this way: life, for instance; some things end this way: life, for instance.

Because some things on the outside want to work their way back into the inside, the essay wants to say so much more, but the writer doesn't know if it is yet safe to.

Sometimes, they will come to visit you one last time in dreams. When my aunt, who also lived in *mueng nogk*, died, she came to my mother in a dream. She said, let's go shopping for sexy clothes; my mother drove her to the shopping mall that turned out to be an airport. Okay, my aunt said, I'm not shopping, I'm really flying away, I'm going home now, I just wanted for you to be the one to take me there.

My mother's wings, I've always taken to mean the wings of a jet plane; or maybe her gumption, her bravery to leave her mother, to run away; or maybe, her bravery to leave her country, go outside to *mueng nogk*.

The little girl wants to go inside. That's why she is crying; we can hear her all night, crying, all night. The family inside the house, they don't want to hear her crying — that's why they are playing their music so loudly. They'll scare her spirit away. Maybe she'll think they've forgotten about her, and then she'll leave. They're so quiet inside the house; maybe she won't hear them; maybe she'll think that they too have all gone away.

I promised myself that I would never tell my mother how I felt about her mother. My mother loved her mother, did everything for her mother; my whole childhood felt as if it was a rehearsal to meet this grandmother. In my childhood home, she hung in the air as if she lived there. Here in *mueng Thai*, no one sleeps anymore in the room she slept in.

My mother says that she will change her name. That is what

she will do when she goes to Thailand again. Because she has no sons, her nephews are becoming monks for her, so that when she dies, she will have that extra help in navigating her way to heaven. My mother says that it isn't fair that she was given a name that means the saddest name, the name of something going away, leaving forever. When her father died, she was given this sad name.

We placed paper flowers on top of the little girl's casket; these, you see, will be the kindling; we said good-bye with a *wai*; we told her spirit to go on, to move on from this life; we washed our hands with holy water in case something crept out to us from the crematorium while we lingered there.

Some things move like this, from whiteness to blackness, from promise to dread — love, for instance; or, writing for instance. In this case, shouldn't I insist on *life* and mean *life*? The sky, so lovely, so lush, so full of blue and light and the swollen life of clouds now creeping, now darkening, now threatening, now loud and thundering. The sky, so calm and promising, now full of sharp, serrated light, a black mood that moves through and scares the water buffalo, the very death owls, into hiding. Even the magnificent sky dragon dare not flit when the sky is like this. And so, the white crematorium sometimes too sends black ash out into the sky to descend upon our lives.

And once, my aunt saw her sitting up in her bed. And once, my nephew saw her walking about the outside of the house, demanding that he climb up and get her some mangoes. And once, my mother saw her standing in the kitchen. And once, someone saw all the lights on in the house and the house was full of strangers and there was so much noise and no one was home. (Mother said that she must have invited all of her friends and family, all of those she knew.) And once, I saw her old wheelchair move. And once, her photograph had a strange look. And once, all the lights went out, but only our house. And once, my sister dreamt that she was unhappy and in one of her moods, just sitting there and staring. And once, a new baby kept crying until it left the house. And once, she kept us up all night going through bags and closets and drawers — we knew it was her by the sound her one good leg made. And once, the dog started to bark at something midair, something that, to us, wasn't there.

My grandmother's ashes were not scattered. They were buried in her urn on the grounds of the village temple. Before we left, we visited her. We brought her money, orchids, tobacco, betel nut, rice, something sweet. We lit incense and candles; we kneeled and greeted her with a *wai*. Instead of a name and the dates of her death and birth, a photograph of her is on the urn. My mother says that sometimes, Yai's face looks happy, and othertimes, she says, it looks sad. That's how we can tell how Yai is feeling, she says. Today, my mother says, Yai's face looks a *little* happy. Everywhere we look, there are green mountains, banana leaves, bamboo trees, grasses blowing in the wind, clouds so low they scuttle almost overhead. These things make you believe in heaven.

In dreams, my ancestors have yellow and long fingernails. Before I can see them, I hear them scraping at wood, at rocks, at windows, at the in between. They hide in dark corners. They crouch. Their eyes, yellow and glowing tiger-like, is what gives them away. (The essay wants to take its time, wants to tell you *everything* about this other life of mine, but the writer wants to finish, wants for the dreams to go away. You see, sometimes, the essay and the writer are not one and the same.) They seem not to understand that once written, they have no way of retracting what has been given life, what has moved from the *inside* into the *outside*; they seem to think that if they threaten me, if they come to me, if they touch me with their long fingernails while I dream, then all this writing of mine will go away, will vanish. Do they not want for any of this, for any of us to rise out of Korat's red dust and trace a passage upon the earth?

Please look, but don't touch, my mother prays.

Before the mark of the monsoon season, when the monks sequester themselves with learning, there is a ceremony that honors the dead. The whole village comes together for this. And because everyone here seems to be my cousin in some way, we are all, in a way, praying to the same ancestors. We bring the monks gifts — things that they will need for the next three months: candles, matches, containers for food and water, toilet paper, towels, flip-flops, soap, laundry detergent, instant noodles, ointments, mosquito coils, all gift-wrapped in a bathing bucket.

    We bring orchids to our ancestors; we light candles and incense. The monks chant, and then we are invited to chant with

them. With one hand, we *wai* our ancestors, and with the other, we touch the back of a relative with our fingertips until we are all connected, our spirits all joined together, one slithering snake. Right now, I think, we are in *mueng Thai*, but there is also *mueng nogk*. I see the lives about me, but all I can think of are those other two dimensions, the outside countries — the back of the snake, whence life comes, and the head of the snake, whither life goes — and knowing that I too am heading toward that space, that seemingly empty space that I *wai* toward with one hand while my other hand desperately tries to touch the life in front of me.

Funeral flowers; crematorium smoke; rice; the iridescent, speckled geckos; jasmine blooms; the underside of the oyster mushroom; the village of the waterfalls of white; the newborn calf; the casket of the little girl; lotus flesh, lotus seeds — the sudden need to, once more, catalog white things before reaching the conclusion to the essay.

Heraclitus said that in the afterlife, our souls will learn to navigate a space that is dark and moist. Moist things smell more than things that are not; our souls, he said, will be moist and we will smell one another. If you wait too long, my aunt says, if you go too late in the day, the mushrooms will have withered, will have gone away, will have retreated back into their damp and dank soil.

Instead of kissing one another on the cheek, in Thailand, we smell one another's cheek. This *home* signifies intense friendship, intense love.

Some things exist this way, in the body of the snake: life, for instance; the essay, for instance. The essay wants to live forever, so too does the writer. In this respect, the essay and writer are one and the same. I will tell you that the essay had a life before this life, and in its current life, that is to say, in the life when it is *alive*, in the *inside*, it is allowed to touch the life around it (dear reader, you), and after it has gone, after it has ended with its last period, it will have another, anterior life.

At any ceremony, the monks will unravel a white string; it will keep going and going and going.

The essay will wonder what could have happened if it had not died. The essay says *someday, if only*. The essay too will, later, much later, want to change its name.

I liked school, my mother said.

I am past the marrying age, my Thai family says; I'm like a stick on a tree that has chosen to grow another way. And I wonder, who will, in the end, when I take my place within the eternal serpent, reach out to touch *me*?

Despite the bad dreams, despite the creaking, despite the smell of something rotting in the air, the writer says, I will let the story of Korat be told. The writer knows that in this life and the next, she will have a lot of spirits with which to contend. The essay says, I will protect you; I will be your talisman.

The essay doesn't seem to understand that, once written, it has no way of retracting what has been given life, what has moved from the *inside* into the *outside*. There were, in this space, in this whiteness, too many spirits who begged to be let in.

But she will be back; she will fly back and forth, back and forth: some things navigate space this way: the essay, for instance; love, for instance. But she will be back; she will fly back and forth, back and forth: I've always taken this to mean that my mother would keep visiting her mother, flying back and forth from *mueng Thai* to *mueng nogk*; or maybe, flying back and forth from this life to the next, this life to the next.

One night, it's so hot the hold of sleep will not take. There are no sounds of tamarind trees rustling, no bamboo branches scraping, no birdsong of the *jingjoke* gecko, no tokay cry breaking the night, just sirens, a plane descending, an occasional drunk man's ramblings. I have orchids growing in my apartment; they hardly spring to life with new buds, with new leaves. My love, my life, my soul turns to me and says, you know, we will never be young again. This makes me weep.

ESSAY ON MY LIFE AS
CATHERINE DENEUVE

IRONY IS NOT ENOUGH:
ESSAY ON MY LIFE AS
CATHERINE DENEUVE

IRONY IS NOT ENOUGH:
ESSAY ON MY LIFE AS
CATHERINE DENEUVE

ANNE CARSON

FALL 1997

saison qui chante saison rapide

I. *Beginnings*

Beginnings are hard.
Sappho put it simply.
Speaking of a young girl Sappho said, *You burn me.*

The woman imagines
herself and the girl
together in a hotel room. But cannot imagine what they would say.

Perhaps she would brush
as if by accident
her backbone. When (later) she is seated in her professor's chair

surrounded by seminar students
listening to her expound
Solonian monetary reform, this accidental brushing action

races on her nerves
like a bit of electricity.
What is interesting about Solon's reform of Athenian money

is that Solon introduced a coinage
which had a forced currency.
That is, citizens had to accept issues called drachmas, didrachmas,

obols, etc.
although these did not contain
silver of that value. These are token coinages.

This is money
that lies about itself
The surface does not match what is going on inside.

The surface (for example) does not
stream with bits of fire.
The girl is one of the students in the seminar. She usually comes late.

II. *Years*

Years later
she will remember
apples splitting open inside her. But the fact is she sits

in a dark church
trying to listen
to an old priest shouting like a treetop. *Devils!* he shouts.

Desire! He shouts.
Pluck your
garment of flesh! Blueblack heat *is — error!*

III. *Days*

Days when the girl does not
show up for the seminar,
blockages of ice form along the woman's veins. She sits

at the head
of the seminar
table under the neon ceiling, under the shadowless hands of the hours

stretching ahead
that lack her.
The seminar meets MonWedFri. This is Mon.

Forty-seven hours until Wed.
The woman unclenches her hands
from her lecture notes and begins to talk. Fragment I of Sappho

has been described by scholars
as a hymn.
Or a parody of a hymn. Or literary use of the hymn form.

Or the literary use
Of the parody
of a hymn. Genuine? Droll? Solemn? Conventional? Hot? Private?

It is a poem
about an old person
who loves a young one. The young one says No and the pain

shines like nails.
Sappho calls out
to Aphrodite who was herself once caught in a gold cage.

But Aphrodite is immortal.
Her smile is immortal.
She flashes it. She mentions justice. And she is gone.

Sappho stands alone
at the end of the poem
under the neon lights with both hands raised. *Here!*

she cries
after the goddess.
Loose me! You! Sappho is nailed to a moment in time.

Aphrodite,
Far off by now
on her chariot of whirring sparrows, looks back and sees

human time
as a system
of perpetual patterns of recurrence. *Don't worry!*

(calls Aphrodite)
The wheel is turning!
Someday your beloved will grow old like you

and love
someone else
who is cold — *I call that justice!* The woman is asking

the students
if they know
a Ray Charles song called *Here We Go Again* when the girl

slouches in
mumbling *Sorry*
as she brushes past and sits on the left. Heat

distresses
that side
of the woman's body Seminar is almost over.

She shuffles her notes
and hastens to conclude,
the eyes beating on her like a wind. Bell rings.

Everyone is rustling
and rising
and shrugging on coats. An earnest boy pins her

with a question
about epithets.
Aphrodite "of the painted chair"? Aphrodite "of the spangled mind"?

Aphrodite "who loves laughter"?
"who loves genitalia"?
(the etymology is disputed) and before she can finish

with epithets
the girl is gone.
Edge of her glance as she slides out the door. Forty-six hours.

IV. *Parts*

Parts of time fall on her
and she does not apprehend them
on the days inbetween MonWedFri. Snow wanders slowly

through the afternoon.
The woman sits in her office
working on an essay about Sokratic irony. Dark blue darkness

grows down
gradually over the snow,
then starlight. She switches off the lamp. Sokrates

uses "irony"
to draw a veil over
the question that is jutting out from him. The veil

is made of feints
and lesser proofs
and half-burnings. Why not just ask the question?

She rises from the desk
and goes out,
closing the office door behind her. Any particular fantasy

about the girl
gets tiresome (she notices)
after 30 minutes. Then she has to elaborate or move on.

Mother I cannot
work the loom
(Sappho says in a fragment). *Aphrodite has parted me*

with longing
for a girl.
The woman is turning over this translation in her mind

when she realizes
she has ridden
the train 4 stops in the wrong direction. I will imagine

a great many things,
she thinks,
climbing back up the stairs from the platform, and none

of them
will happen.
Other things will happen. Her hip slams hard into the metal arm

of the turnstile.
A red sign
pasted on it says NO EXIT.

Sound is far away.
All around her
strange lamps burn brightly and human tongues press the night.

V. *Awake*

Awake too early
and dry from fantasy
the woman lies on herbed under the window. Stares out

at the stale 4 AM sky.
No help there.
Switches on the bedside lamp. Its greenish glare

shows a Lobel edition
of Sappho
lying open on the floor. Fragment 58 is a torn 3rd-century papyrus:

> *by mouth*
> *beautiful gifts girls*
> *songlover lyreclear*
> *all my skin old age already*
> *white becomes the hair after black*
> *knees do not carry*
> *like fawns*
> *but what could Ido?*
> *not able to become*
> *dawn with arms of roses*
> *ends of the earth carries*
> *takes*
> *deathless one in the bed*
> *contemplates*
> *but I love delicacy and this to me*
> *this bright thing of the sun this beautiful thing*
> *Eros has allotted*

The woman closes
the book.
Outside ice is general. Say someone had it, the courage.

VI. *Weekends*

Weekends are long and white.
Snow drifts against the door.
Distant threads from the piano downstairs. Footsteps creak

back and forth
across the ceiling.
The woman slides slowly from hour to hour, tracing

with one vague finger
at the back of her mind
the girl, on the other side of the city moving parallel to herself

through these same hours.
She reads. Writes. Eats.
Answers the telephone. Sleeps. Wakes. Folds up

sleeping bag.
Checks the ice.
Starts over. So does the other, somewhere.

On the big map
of the untraceable world event
two parallel red lines, of differing lengths,

inch forward
a weekend's worth of lifetime,
not touching. Chalices ripen in the shadow do they not.

VII. *Shame*
Shame too
is a relation.
That fact that the girl has been absent from the seminar

for a week now
is a rusty edge
that the woman collides with repeatedly as she sits in her

Monday office
paging through
lecture notes and looking out on snowstreaked slate roofs.

A flag shreds itself
in the icy wind.
Telephone rings. Jagged pause. Girl's voice,

which she has
never heard before
on the telephone, is surprisingly dark and a little wild.

Animal lopes through her
and turns at the wall.
Claws rake it. *Not coming to the seminar today. Thought you*

should know.
Girl stops.
She waits. And then, *Do you care?* with a torn laugh.

Stairs
drop away
from the woman's life. Dangling and lightless she grabs for an answer

to that.
Yes. No.
No answer. Wrong answer. Wrong question. Trick question!

They grapple
in the void,
firing badly. It spins, they slip off, then hold.

I plan to come
Wednesday,
girl says. *Do that*, she answers. Dial tone.

The world sags
and swings back
against the rock at the middle of the void. Fifty-two hours.

VIII. *Presence*

Presence can be
like a sunset
that breaks open. They sit opposite one another in her office.

Colors flood
in a backrush
from the bookshelf to the desk, up the wall and down the other side.

Hard work
keep the conversation
steady on school matters — to the girl likes digressions:

about boyfriends
(two,
in different cities) and her theory of monogamy

(its folly) and
A judgment
of now *(You're someone I talk to)*.

Phrases from this conversation
will stream past the woman's mind
for days and nights after. *Life is really very simple.*

The door closes behind her.
Blood is jumping.
She tries to read, eats a carrot, rips up something, goes out.

Over snowdrifts
to the church
The priest is putting ashes on foreheads. Light oily pressure

of his thumb
on her brow
makes her begin to weep. Little red thread jerks the raw heart alive

IX. *Damaged*

Damaged crop — what
the body brings in
through its double lens of living and watching oneself live.

The girl stops her
on her way to the seminar.
Do you mind if I come to class when I haven't prepared the text?

Rage spins her.
Another trick question.
No, she says coldly. Fawns are made of lies! Who

is immoral
in this fluidity
of inside and outside? Who could tell,

reading this,
that she was
not even one step ahead of it? Trick questions

(she notes in passing)
have a structure
akin In Sokratic irony. Why this calms her she cannot say.

X. *Reading*
Reading Week means 7 days
of no girl.
She sits in her office till evening working on irony. Blueblackness

pools in the air.
Lights come on
All over the city. *Free as a flame that devours* is how

one German philosopher
describes the irony
of Sokrates, moving over human errors and human knowledge.

To swap a Yes for a No
is its action,
he says. Sokrates might have enjoyed a girl who told him

Life is really very simple.
Who knew how to run
knife after knife along the edge. A cold rarity like blue peaches

is soaking
out of the sunset.
Evening you bring back to me (says Sappho) *everything*

dispersed by dawn.
Sappho was one
who understood how simple life is. And she was unsurprised

when certain people
became for her,
by their very existence, a trick question. Sappho

called these people
fawns.
The woman faces into clearing winds all the way home. Ice

going black
underfoot — what
is that smell? — it comes stinging into her,

sudden bitter memory
of pushing her face
hard into the black leather shoulder of a girl,

hipbone grinding her hipbone,
under a streetlamp
one cold February night years ago. How simply time carries us.

A familiar block
thuds into place
in her chest as she climbs the stairs to her house. Inside

it is dark.
The floors are silent.
Moonlight slides in. Voices of the world grow fewer and quieter

XI. *Snows*

Snows all night
snows all day.
Still snowing in midafternoon when the woman looks up

from her Greek lexicon.
The girl's ears
are bright red. Eyebrows snowplastered. She leans

in the doorway
and holds up
her glasses by one broken earpiece. She accepts

the mending tape,
mends the earpiece,
drops her coat on the floor, sits beside it. Takes out

her Greek book
and they begin
to translate, as if it had been prearranged. Had it?

The woman feels like
something hooked
or washing out to sea, but the force of life coming off this girl

is too strong
to think what
day it is or what was supposed to happen. Dusk reaches

them.
She switches on
the desklamp. But now the girl is lifting her coat,

in the doorway,
gone.
Thanks, floats back along the hall. Looking down

she sees
her feet
are naked. Boots and socks propped on the radiator to dry.

How strange
to have read Greek
barefoot with a girl in a snowstorm, how strangely burning.

XII. *Tools*
Tools of the educator include
repetition and irony.
The woman sits in her small night kitchen working over

an ancient fragment
of the poet Alkaios
who lived in the 7th century BC and wrote many pages

(most of them lost)
about the hungering
haze of desire, unto which no fortress is secure, no wall avails:

> *me wretched me the whole of evils sharing*
> *in my house*
> *shameful lot*
> *for incurable maiming comes upon me*
> *and the belling of a deer inside my chest*
> *grows in its fears*
> *going mad*
> *by reason of infatuations*

Why study the past?
To illumine the present.
Why study the present? The woman is groping as mortals do

to get hold of
the edge of
herself in time. In time. You have to repeat the important words

until you
understand them.
Amid this indignity, in this ridiculous late fire, without

wall or fortress
or food to stop
the belling of the deer, she is struggling to see it lit

by whatever floods
the momentarily
open lens — an old woman's love is a coin

rattling
in an empty cup
making the sound KISHKUSH. The pandering stars look down.

XIII. *Truth*
Truthfully white is Friday.
Marchblasted open on raw winds.
Quite early the girl arrives at her office, closes the door

and starts to cry.
Is having trouble
with her boyfriend in Paris. Most important

thing in her life.
This, the girl adds,
gesturing toward the woman's books, chairs, shelves

and desklamp,
is the second most important.
The woman nods. Painful to see the girl cry but in truth

she can hardly
feel anything
above the blast of happiness this presence affords.

Fire is ripping
inside.
She presses both hands on her chest. Murmurs a phrase of comfort.

The girl moves stiffly to the door,
knocks over a chair
with her knee and leaves. She sits. Wheels of hot magma

are riding
up the pipes
and want out. Do you know how diamonds get to us?

Three hundred miles
underground
are heats and pressures that crush carbon

into sparkling shapes.
These are driven
to the surface along volcanic corridors called diamond pipes

and extruded
onto a crater
at the top. The journey may take months

or days
or hours.
No human has ever witnessed a diamond eruption. For reasons

that elude science
diamond pipes are found only
in the most ancient volcanic regions. No crater less than 1.5

billion years old
will give you
a diamond. So long it takes to make a beautiful thing

out of interior fire.
Later in the seminar
she avoids looking at the girl's red eyes. And after class

when she comes
to her office
it is pure pain — there she sits telling of her love

in Paris
while the woman nods
and tries to force her lungs closed — uprush of diamonds

shearing
the breath off.
If I could just be in the same room with him! the girl is saying

and the woman
turns to stare hard
out the window where deep blue night dye has begun

to saturate
everything.
The girl is lifting her coat. *Gottago.*

Pauses.
Turns.
You help. I don't know how. She is gone.

The desklamp
sputters, goes
out. The woman is lacing on her big boots for the long walk home.

XIV. *Sokrates*

Sokrates died in jail.
Sappho died in a leap
off the white rock of Leukas for love of a girl, so they say.

Sokrates is ironical
about two things.
His beauty (which he calls ugliness) and his knowledge

(ignorance).
For Sappho
irony is a verb. It places her in a certain relation

to her own life.
Silk and bitter.
How very interesting (the woman thinks) to watch myself

construct this.
She is at work
on her essay. *Irony contains and excites a feeling of insoluble*

opposition
between
the unconditional and the conditional,

between what
it is impossible
and what it is necessary to say, says the German

Philosopher
Schlegel.
Latin rhetoricians translate the Greek word *eironia* as

dissimulatio,
which means
"mask." Just so (Sappho notes) in time

one's mask
becomes
one's face. *Irony is no joke*, Schlegel warns her. A miniature

smoke of grief
climbs
her throat and escapes into the room, turning dark

now and sulphurous
in the confused
ash of evening, in the drifting ash alone. *With the best*

will in the world
I believe that
I would only, make myself ridiculous! remarked Sokrates ironically.

XV. *Poor*
Poor idea this girl fantasy,
the woman is thinking
as she packs up after the Friday seminar. Girl has missed

the last three
assignments.
Bare clarities of March afternoon ache in through the wide glass

of her window.
The big boots
feel like two tombstones. Then unexpectedness happens.

Ducking out the main door
onto the street
she stumbles against the girl rushing in. Girl thrusts

today's assignment at her.
Glad I caught you, she says.
The woman pulls her eyes away. Folds the assignment twice.

Pushes it down
in her briefcase.
Cannot think of a thing to say. The world is like champagne,

crosses her mind
as they circle
one another in the doorway in a wash of light. Girl is looking

at her oddly.
*Never saw you
in this state before*, she says. *What state is that?*

Tongue-tied, the girl grins.
The woman has
a sensation of being flicked on a hook.

Eyes grip
and untie.
The girl starts to talk about her love in Paris

who thinks her
too dependent.
You? the woman says, hitting the bottom of a volcanic pipe

at top speed,
all her diamonds
going the wrong way. The girl touches her arm and departs.

Later at home
the woman sits
by a dark open window. Smell of night so different

than smell of day.
Frozen darkness
like old tin. Like cold cats. Like the word *pauvre*.

XVI. *Questions*

Questions are not all tricks,
are they?
The woman gives a dinner party for the seminar students.

She cooks
all day
while fantasies of herself and the girl fill every room.

Hot stones
murmur, hiss,
dash, churn and clatter upon one another then drop

perpendicularly
back
to the molten conical mount forming at the pit of her lungs.

It is a snowy spring evening.
Night comes.
The students arrive. They pile up plates of food. They pour

glasses of wine
and sit on the floor
and say miraculous things. She watches each one. She

waits.
She sips.
Night moves on its way. The food is all over the room,

then gradually disappears.
The students gather
and separate and regather in different doorways,

then they too gradually
disappear.
It is almost 2 AM when she closes the door and switches off

the porchlight
and returns
slowly along the hall. Out the window she can see

snow flying
diagonally
under the yellow streetlamp. The woman folds her

trick question
back up into
her heart and closes it. Why had it not occurred to her

that the girl
just
wouldn't show up? Life is, as she says, simple.

The woman almost laughs.
Begins picking up cups
and plates and odd bits of food. Puts away chairs.

Blows out
candles.
Lines up bottles beside the door. Loads the dishwasher

and sits down
to watch
the rest of the night go by. *Everything*, she says to herself

as darkness turns
to red fog along the hall,
Everything we can think of to fend off decay just warms the pearls.

XVII. *Weaponry*

Weaponry is her subject
on Monday
when the girl flashes into the seminar 20 minutes late and sits

on the left.
Out the side
of her eye she can see she is white-faced, uncombed,

shirt half tucked
in and half out.
She continues to speak about hoplite armour of the 7th century BC.

The class
is sleepy.
They are reading a poem of Alkaios about a silent room.

Plumes nod mutely
from helmets
nailed to roofbeams. Greaves hang brilliant and motionless

on pegs
along the wall.
Tunics and hollow shields are piled on the floor beside heaps

of breastplates
and belts and
Khalkidian swords. So says Alkaios. *Why is he telling us this?*

the woman asks.
No one
answers. Not a bee buzzes. Haunted old phrases

stare up at them
from the book.
What — she begins but the girl interrupts. *It's about a war*

not happening.
She turns.
Their eyes thwack in midair. *That's right,*

the woman says.
Nothing is happening.
The bell rings. She leaves the room without looking back.

XVIII. *Desire*

Desire historically
is not a choice.
A girl, a deer, a woman, ropes — all day Thursday she

sits grading
midterm exams
(girl failed) and observing desire's ropes within her,

what frail
strips
they are, just strikings of light really. Girl will never know

this half-life
they lived
together in the complicated lake. By the irony of the lake

every rope doubles.
Every love halves.
But the woman is aware of a cold rusty smell. She is

tightening
the ropes
herself. This girl is already stale in her. And what feels wrong

now, as she
looks at it,
is the shamelessly general nature of desire. It blows

through the body
like a sunset wind.
Slant and childlike errors (for example, this girl)

reveal themselves,
but the immensity
of the wind does not abate, nor our sense of bending to it

as roots
bend
in the dark underground, blindly and heavily

toward some
smell of light
that drops down matter — who can claim to have chosen love?

XIX. *Counterlight*
Counterlight is
flooding the room
when the woman arrives on Friday. A note is stuck

under her door.
From some
student who says she can't come

to the seminar
today. *But at 5 PM*
I would like to see you scrawled on a page torn out of

Der Spiegel
showing
Ingeborg Bachmann playing chess. The woman studies

Ingeborg
Bachmann
whose wonderful clear gaze falls straight down on

the little knight
at the center of
her gameboard. Whose shiny bangs are those of a 9-year-old girl,

swept by hand
to the left.
Whose smile is immortal. Due to strengthening thoughts of

Ingeborg
Bachmann's
bangs, the woman is able to conduct an allusive and slightly

sarcastic seminar
at top speed on
fragment 286 of Ibykos. She discourses calmly

on male desire
and female
desire, the difference. Ibykos describes a springtime garden

of watered boughs
and uncut girls.
Time holds them deep in its amorous pinch, soaked buds

of pure use
as female
clockwork goes. But what is this black thing that comes

parching
down
like lightning out of a north wind from Thrace: Eros has

neither season
nor reason (so
Ibykos claims) in a man's life. Male desire is gears gone mad

anywhere
anytime
without warning or water it shatters his lungs.

"Lungs"
stands
in manly exposure as the last word of the poem. The woman gives

a short
summary
of ancient respiratory theory, avoiding the gaze

of the girl
who today
is seated directly across the table from her, wearing

a new
silver
earring. *Thank you*, she says after the girl translates

a Greek phrase
with extreme
vulgarity, making the others laugh. At the bell

the girl leaves
abruptly.
She packs up her books as the room empties. Farcical,

she thinks,
is the life
of desire and yet — access to the human may be rare enough

to justify
it, overall.
She sits down and leans her head on the table and starts to laugh.

At any rate
it is good
to exercise the lungs from time to time. Is it not Sappho who says:

> *not decay nor rust*
> *nor shadow*
> *not winds nor fear*
> *nor failure of winds*
> *not silence*
> *nor sleep not betrayal*
> *can pull my heart away*
> *from praising*
> *the beautiful thing that love was*
> *when love was the world*

Late and deep
the woman goes
back down the hall. Inside her office the light is stopped silver,

old ice of April
unlacing its fast. She turns,
hearing the bell ring 5 o'clock. Comes a knock at the door.

DIVISION

DIVISION

DIVISION

DIVISION

DIVISION

KATIE FORD

SPRING 2004

We drove through Wyoming passing people on horseback, noon horse shadows like those of caskets lifted up, the dead sitting up through pine boxes, looking at the strange reins in their hands. Once we were in the mountains we saw no animals, no birds. Green signs beside the granite rocks dated them back to the Triassic Age, Mississippian. On the opposing hill, the trail the goats wore down coming to water curved like a strand of hair, a single hair, unmassed. You said stop the car. Look at that, you said, pointing at the strips of ice-age rock, settling. A mountain range is simply a crease in the land is how it was taught to me. A crease is the foresight of division, you were taught. Desperate for communion, Catherine of Siena was beside herself in hills like these, eating nothing but an herb she would suck on and spit out. She scalded herself at the baths, ran away to a cave, shoved twigs into her mouth so that when the host traveled down her raw throat she would indeed feel something, even a god breaking inside her. Would you look at that, you said again near the rail of the viewpoint, where the historical marker explained the plates underneath. Beneath it, a crow's wing. Lord of confusion, Lord of great slaughter and thin birds, you could never answer all of us at once. Layer by layer I imagined pulling it apart to find the upholding musculature beneath the soot and grease of flight. Finding none — just the spinelike axis and its branching barbs, minute hooks holding them together — we continued on to the hotel parking lot in Sheridan, where at night someone scraped a key or a knife alongside the car while we slept off what we could. It was hard to tell what was used. There was nowhere to fix it. There was no talk of ever fixing it.

EXCERPTED FROM
THE DARK BURTHEN

EXCERPTED FROM
THE DARK BURTHEN

EXCERPTED FROM
THE DARK BURTHEN

EXCERPTED FROM
THE DARK BURTHEN

MICHAEL IVES

SPRING 2012

The eye is not satisfied with seeing.
— Ecclesiastes 1:8

Feb 4 "Units" of feces, their pinched ends all elegantly aligned, as if by design, arranged at the throat of the toilet like a bunch of root vegetables, and then I flush and they explode and are sucked away.

Feb 6 Unremarkable, except for the ragged side of one stool, which called to mind the surface of a wood rasp. The edge of a turd is the original Barbary coast.

Feb 25 One rather long and almost perfectly straight cylinder, pinched off at the end like an elongated silicone crystal from an extrusion device prior to being sliced into super-conducting wafers. Quite elegant, though painfully discharged. Reading from Goncourt's journals the while.

Mar 1 Immense heap of feces discharged just now, the summit of which rose at least an inch above the level of the water, like a great igneous mound along the Pacific Ring of Fire. Two-stage flushing required, in the intermission of which, while searching for a nail clipper in the upper vanity drawer, discovered a sample-size deodorant with a scent called "Sports Meadow."

Mar 4 Volcanic explosion this morning, courtesy of last night's shiraz, dark and disheveled, like yew bushes. *A crank topiary obscures the DMV.*

Mar 7 Frighteningly blonde excreta this morning, which must be the result of Trevor's peculiar laxative recipe. Was reminded of Johnny Winter. And Yellow Man. But who are the great albino jazz musicians?

Mar 8   Read through several pages on the *Ismaili Order of the Assassins* while "discharging my Body of that uneasy Load." Produced an undistinguished several small, thin tubules the color of sorrel leaves when they die. That the word "assassin" is derived from "hashish" has to be the most tiresome of all the etymological "wonders."

Mar 14 Two or three anonymous, kibble-like pellets which, when I flushed, circled each other momentarily like sparks above a campfire before submitting to their inexorable journey toward the septic tank.

Mar 28 This morning an heliacal twist with a . . . of smaller dollops nested in the interior of it. Looked something like a pregnant gyroscope. When I depressed the flush handle, the works toppled over on its side and disappeared into the throat of the toilet.

Apr 2   See Giacometti's "Woman with Her Throat Cut" (or perhaps some sort of instrument of torture) and recall last night's impression: that E.'s cocktail conversation was drawing naïve guests into Maiden of Nuremberg–type traps of intellectual ambush from which they didn't recover for the rest of the evening.

Apr 8   I see a hydraulic jack resting lightly on the Virgin Islands.

Apr 10 Like the clown at a state fair birthing center muttering to himself, "Focus, focus, damn it," I did manage to force an enormous set of luggage through the portal just now — rectilinear, remote, like half-submerged inscrutable monoliths at the mouth of a harbor, for which municipal tour guides offer competing explanations. The image of an ibis-headed driver's ed instructor continues to haunt me.

Apr 11 Another spiral this morning, unbroken, oriented at a 45-degree angle to the throat of the toilet with the upper surface of one of the loops cresting above the waterline. A texture so smooth, I was barely aware of the emission. Imagining someone with such exquisite control over his sphincter that he could "turn" his stool as if on a wood lathe.

Apr 12 Read this morning from Moore's *A Dictionary of Geography*, . . . in distinction from the *Fumarole*, the exhalations from the solfatara consist principally of sulphuretted hydrogen and other sulphurous gases." My urine smells like burning papyrus.

Apr 14 Delicious crème brûlée at Hattie's last night. We dropped martinis from the roof garden. Revealed to R. and P. the rudiments of a copro-poesis. They had at the ready, as always, numerous precedents and ripostes. Artaud was mentioned, of course, and Michel Tournier. We smoked. No matter the regularity of my bowel movements (every morning after coffee), nicotine always produces an immediate laxative effect. Upon entering the men's room, I encountered a large man with a deformed ear waving his hands in front of the motion sensor on the paper towel dispenser (unfortunate rhyme) as though he were playing a theremin.

Apr 16 Unbroken coil of feces this morning, which reminded me immediately of the snake on the California state flag. Dropped a single square of toilet paper onto it, watched the lineaments of the coil slowly emerge, as if from behind a rice paper screen, then flushed away the works.

Apr 19 Immense discharge this morning, with peaks rising above the surface of the water in arrangements of considerable complexity, as of coral atolls in the Pacific. Presently I ruminate on the alleged translocation of the Islands of the Blessed, in a feverish but futile effort to escape the insufferable dignity of their inhabitants. Io and her fly, the Islands of the Blessed and the blessed, Prius man and his caca.

Apr 20 I see a broken sextant, but itself composed (loosely) of a broken ankh, a broken spoon, a broken shackle, and a broken taproot.

May 8 While at the park, let loose a warrior king's tirade into the plastic basin of the Porta-John. From outside it must have sounded like the cosmic sow slumbering in a gelatin mold.

May 9 Single large sea-cucumber, dendrochita to be precise — like a length of Polish sausage terminating in a tuft of respiratory trees. Half expected it, hung over as I am, to follow me around the house.

May 15 Perfectly immobile, mildly odoriferous stool this morning — innocuous really, yet invested with a terrible significance. I wouldn't think of probing it manually, though it might carry news of my imminent demise. This silent Bartleby-like mass, at once both sinister and meaningless — it calls to mind M's latest graphic novel, the flesh eaters

of which she has elected to equip with peonies for heads, and not the cypripedium, or lady's slipper orchid, that I had proposed. "Not the cypri-
pedium?" I said to her incredulously by phone the other morning, "even though the labellum, or lip, of that flower resembles the grossly oversized chin of a hideous alien and often appears to have veins running through it?" But she said she'd conducted informal "focus groups" and carried out research that vindicated her theoretical surmise — that an aberrant plasticity of association lurks beneath apparently stable categories of thought. Like huge canines inside a stupid cluster of petals, blood in the stool of a color-blind man.

May 17 Neatly kerfed cylindrical modules of stool later this afternoon. Has my sphincter become a Play-Doh extrusion toy?

May 25 To the degree that they abhor it, men wash themselves in shit. As one defecates into the same circling waters, other and still other waters circle beneath one.

May 27 (Copromancy.)

May 28 Sunburst of rheumy floatage, as of a child's vomit — the larger elements disposed near the center with coronal flares of finer stuff circumjacent.

Jun 3 Magmatic and prolific.

Jun 8 Too soon I shall enter my second infancy, and the bowel's berry shall then mingle with the linen.

Jun 9 Recalled yesterday my boyhood neighbor, Cents, who badgered me for over a year to sing with his barbershop chorus. He must have been in his early forties at the time, I fourteen or fifteen. The rehearsals were held an hour and a half east, in _____, known chiefly for its maximum security prison. As Cents drove, he would alternate between jokes about the nature of vaginas and discussion of a family disease with which he was stricken, a disease that required that his colon be catheterized such that he had, in his words, "to shit out of the side of his body," which image made me shudder within. "They sewed up the asshole God bequeathed me and tapped another one upstream," I distinctly remember him saying. I was utterly mystified by the remark. During

one rehearsal he let on that he had once witnessed a fight between my parents and considered getting involved but didn't, thinking it somehow inappropriate to interrupt my father while he "took care of his business." "Is your father a fag, do you think?" Cents would ask me on a regular basis, as if I thought this supposition humorous. He joked that perhaps I might arrange a date for him with my mother. "She's one hotty," Cents would remind me as frequently as he offered up observations about his colostomy. In the end I agreed to participate in one public performance with the chorus, at an Elk's Lodge in _____. While we were dressing for the event in the basement boiler room, Cents at last showed me the aperture in his side, after asking with great fanfare if I wanted to see his "asshole." (Strange, I had assumed for some reason that with the closing off of his rectum, his buttocks would have been surgically fused.) "What looks and smells horrible, but feels great?" Cents would ask me repeatedly during drives home from the barbershop chorus rehearsals. I always replied dutifully, "I don't know, what looks and smells horrible, but feels great?" And Cents would answer, "Pussy," and he'd laugh, and I would laugh, but without knowing what I was laughing about. And then invariably Cents would challenge me to a farting contest, pretend to start unbuttoning his shirt, laugh again and ask, "Hey, how about that date with your mother?"

Jun 10   (Underwater ziggurat.)

Jun 4   Chiasmus: the demon shits end-stops of nacre while a black, feculent script passes from between the buttocks of the angel.

Jun 16   Harassed woman metamorphoses into heifer; shrub in flames into voice of god; Indo-European aspirates *bh*, *dh*, and *gh* into voiced plosives *b*, *d*, and *g*, etc.; gentle person into resurrection event; "blah-blah" into "yada-yada"; last night's pot roast into this fuscous, pelican-shaped heap.

Jun 21   On the eve of the summer solstice, the mediums, whose rates of digestion have been closely scrutinized for the preceding several months, are trussed up in an apparatus on a pillar at the center of a lake, their arms extended and open in a supplicative posture, their torsos held aloft by three iron rings, one under the arms, another at midchest; the last supports the buttocks and from this lower ring extend stirrups into which the feet are inserted to hold their legs.

At the appointed time late in the evening before the solstice each is fed a paste of very specific composition containing liberal amounts of gold dust. In the morning a novitiate administers a series of palpitations and auscultations of his abdomen. Near midday the pontifex fits into the medium's anus a collared valve. Directly before the passage of the sun through the solstitial point at the southern Tropic, he is fed, as needed, a mild laxative. The whole of the priestly caste assembles along the shores of the lake. When the sun stands directly overhead, the work of the preceding year comes to fruition: gold coin begins to pour from the anus of the medium as if he were a slot machine. Hence, the mint and treasury of the tribe are at once contained in this excretor of ducats.

Jun 24   Tremendous din of pneumatic billingsgate immediately prior to this morning's evacuation. God, I thought for a minute as though I'd deflate entirely. Mrs. Blickstein upstairs would have found me days later, looking like a flaccid Claes Oldenburg sculpture, draped over the toilet.

Jun 26   Smooth, steep, slightly furrowed cliffs of primary stool with an apron of coarse talus at the base. Begin to think I couldn't manually, with modeling clay, achieve a better facsimile of slide rock formation.

Jun 30   Terrible constipation this morning. Felt as though I was passing a feldspar table radio through the delicate portal.

Jul 8   Very strange dream last night in which I was examining my feces through a magnifying lens somehow fitted into the side of the *sphincter ani externus*, which scrutiny involved a combined 180-degree twist of the torso and dorsal collapse of the spine, both of which I accomplished without any strain whatsoever, though why the dream had me twist around so and not simply bring my head down ventrally between my legs remains a mystery (cf. childhood dreams of self-fellatio). Stranger still the agglomeration of objects in the stool as it passed by the lens: finger cymbals, escapements and tiny gears, radiolarians, damselfly wings, calliope bolts, all trapped in a smooth and accommodating matrix (an unconscious inclination toward pica, perhaps). Then was somehow sitting upright looking into an optometric console as if to be fitted for glasses, except that I was examining my own stool rather than reading off rows of letters. Whenever I moved my face away from the scope I found I was still

lying on the ground contorted as before. An anonymous attendant slid the lenses in and out and asked me what I saw. This person was taking detailed notes and at the same time, or so I intuited, determining the composition of my stool. What appeared at first as the cementing matrix, upon greater magnification, proved to be itself composed of yet more objects. With each increment of magnification, the ratio of matrix to trapped objects decreased until I arrived at what the attendant described as "the shit of the shit," the elements of which fitted together like the tiles in an Escher drawing.

Jul 9   *Evidence suggests that primitive refrigerators walked upright across the plains of New Jersey millions of weeks ago, presumably more adaptable members of the genus ice box, but the fossil record remains murky. Buried in a dark earth equidistant between points and condenser, prodigious coprolites tell us of these roving brutes of the Canarsie period, titans searching for the marrow of men, but when they found it, they called it Pop-Tart.*

Jul 10   Divinities of our psychical moons stir typhonic forces at the center of the aliment, confirmable by this disgusting and voluminous slurry. *Came then the Rhubarb Monsoons.*

Jul 12   In primitive/industrial terms, the defecating animal's anus pictured as an opposed-blade damper, through which the flow of excreta is regulated by means of two ranks of Teflon-coated louvers which, actuated along a common linkage, are arranged such that adjacent blades rotate in contrary directions.

Jul 14   I see a nebular region in the upper-left quadrant, and in the upper right a shag of pope's knuckles cornered in a bay sprig. The rest says nothing to me.

Jul 15   (Compression sutures.)

Jul 16   Jehovah as the eternal two-year-old at play with his feces when by accident, after untold aeons, he happens to fashion a man out of it (think monkeys in a room with typewriters). Being of like substance with its father, the excremental mandrake has no need of a life-giving blast of air and, auto-animated, runs from its maker. God, ever in chase of his gingerbread boy!

Jul 19   Titanic effort this morning to pass what felt like a pier of solid granite extending the length of my descending colon, the force of which nearly blew my eyeballs out of their orbits. A jube of translucent blooms in my vision just after reminded me that perception is a mediated affair.

Jul 20   The Bristol Stool Scale! Abomination of vagueness! A physiognomy of the smiley face captures subtler degrees of nuance.

Jul 24   Shat what looked like the whole of the Carnac Stones this morning, which prolificacy inspired in my mind the fantasy of a tribal mascot who is fed and defecates for years on end and rises with the growing altitude of his self-produced dung heap.

Aug 2   (Cacation.)

Aug 4   Unruly gobbets massed around an irregularly flanged diagonal.

Aug 6   Decanted just now, *molto largo*, a dark and vile grume. My bowel's a viaduct of shame.

Aug 9   Loud, silly voidance about a quarter of an hour ago, all blousy at the bottom, then tapering off, with enlarged headstock, marbled like an Eisenhower-era jaspé linoleum.

Aug 10   The face of the sleeper is the emblem of innocence, but there is another face, which discloses, between its Aeolus cheeks, the all-appropriating event, different from birth, running through it, through all things. *A thiol plume steers the universe.*

Aug 11   Careful footsteps away from a wilderness latrine: petals on this wet black Earth.

Aug 13   My bastard accomplishment, these mute lobes of filth, building their puppet theater for hours inside me.

Aug 16   (Mud room.)

Aug 27   Possible worlds of the philosophers are devoid of excrement because their architects are tissues of refusals.

Aug 28   Happened absently to be opening and closing the van-

ity cupboard door when I noticed that the friction catch (consisting of spring clip + striking loop) and the human rectum/sphincter assembly were more or less homologous (that is, spring clip = rectum, striking loop = stool), but only in gross structure, insofar as while a distension in the walls of the rectum triggers, via stress receptors, the defecation reflex, which relaxes the internal and external sphincters and allows a release of rectal cargo, the two elements of the friction catch are parted by an external force. Expulsion from within vs. extraction from without.

Sep 2   By a serendipitous arrangement of "components," something like the profile of Teddy Roosevelt. I am the heir of Arcimboldo, though I work with a more limited palette.

Sep 3   Carefully laid two pieces of toilet paper torn into triangles on either side of a miniature sea wall of delicate globes and bars: coupling system between the wings of an experimental butterfly.

Sep 4   Disburdened myself of something halfway between a sea anemone and bizarrely crenelled castle turret or Donjon keep. Small cloaklets of bubbles obscured a clear view of its base.

Sep 5   Quick dissipative envelopes of smoke — a geisha's footfalls away from the imperial commode.

Sep 6   (Dung an sich.)

Sep 7   Like a Jules Verne character, tunneling through mantles of excrement in a blood-cooled vehicle toward the diamond core beyond aversion.

Sep 8   Read an article yesterday in the *Times* about ongoing efforts on the West Coast to make sewer water potable. Draining off the little bit of drinkable water from our excrement like bums squeezing alcohol from a handful of Sterno. The Big Bang of civilization retreats back into its anus. Call me the Spengler of dooky.

Sep 9   Time as an invisible worm: its peristalsis is the days, and months and years; its feces physical manifestations. But on what does it feed?

Sep 10 Life shits corpses.

Sep 11   Odd, sea-kale–like heaps this morning. I think of piles of cold dark pajamas in the corner of a recently deceased child's bedroom. I'm a sad old spado, I am.

Oct 7   Nasty gorgon of stool discargoed just now. Resembled a blasted tree stump torn from a cliff's edge.

Oct 11   At nadir and zenith, innocuous spherules, each with a single, sine wave-shaped compression suture, which gives them the appearance of spherical and decrepit yin-yang symbols. In the middle, one fluke of a Danforth anchor resting on the head of a coach bolt with a bit of the shaft remaining. The whole center assembly nosed by small imperfect commas.

Oct 12   Two bollard-shaped masses this morning — rather bollards toppled onto their sides, or winches so toppled. The latent longshoreman in me wanted to belay a length of carpet thread around them.

Oct 15   Children are insensitive to mortality and immortality and thus are closer to immortality, and correlatively, unashamed of their feces. The adolescent, with his taste for heroic krinkle-kut spirituality, fastens, courtesy of a 24-hour hormone parade, to the idea that he will live forever — the debased immortality — but he requires constant ratification in the form of social acceptance, which carries with it the mandate to maintain a strict regimen of hygiene. No one knows what a hygiene detached from ideology would look like, a hygiene practiced solely for the purposes of minimizing disease. The heroic depends on the hygienic. Filth is "not mine." The *Satthipatana Sutta* prescribes long concentrated meditation on charnel grounds and corpses and the noxious vapors circulating just inches away from the *mudra*. Shit interrupts the dissociative dream, even if the interruption is itself only another layer of dream. Shit may be the closest equivalent to the *nunc stans*.

Oct 16   I see nothing, nothing more than filth.

Oct 17   I see filth.

Oct 18   Again, filth.

Oct 20 Okay, a lambda (lower case), the pediment of a bungalow (a stretch), and a short-barreled blow dryer.

Oct 23 By middle age saxophones and oral sex cease to be the ticket to rebellion they once were, as the demands of vocation and diminishing health put a jello-mold over all the old remembered liberties, which jiggle still but are no longer capable of real transport, and one's free time is all that can, but only temporarily, banish the anxiety of shriveling horizons, while small docile explosions in the bowel rearrange to no effect scattered bits of an abiding will to accommodate.

Oct 25 Antefixes, stopcocks, euphoniums.

Oct 26 Desublimation: "Excrement has pitched its mansion in the place of love."

Oct 27 Swollen rolls of cinnamon bark this morning, as of a raft disassembled by cruel seas.

Nov 5 "What can we know of the world?" asks Perec. "What quantity of space can our eyes hope to take in between our birth and our death? How many square centimeters of Planet Earth will the soles of our shoes have touched?" No one would deny these are rhetorical questions, but how many will adjust their ambitions accordingly, how many acknowledge the futility of world travel? I reiterate what the true ascetic realizes: If you want to know the world, circumnavigate your own ejecta.

Nov 6 "It is said that the ordure of the Grand Lama of Thibet was at one time so venerated that it was collected and worn as amulets." Gould and Pyle, *Anomalies and Curiosities of Medicine.*

Nov 4 Grim dalliance of undedicated cleat shapes punctuated and wreathed in bubbles.

Nov 5 Two eels commencing to twine in the act of love (have no idea how eels breed). Their still passion breaks them at the twist point.

Nov 8 Mottled and woundy this morning, like the fur of a vanquished hyena.

Nov 9   As if a murex's egg mass had usurped the central whorls of a rose — the weight of it against a chance disposition of toilet paper forms the outer petals.

Nov 15 In the fascistic order of hygiene, the stool and its associated sensations play the conceptual Jew.

Nov 18 Loamy Capernaum of a discharge just now. Stray unopened tampons and replacement razor handles in the depths of the vanity drawer reminded me of ancient felled trees at the bottom of a river.

Nov 21 Delicate, flame-shaped, numerous: sculpted hyphens between what I've been and what I am.

Nov 22 The anus as articulator, and excrement the speech of physical aliment.

Nov 25 Fuselage of Paleolithic jetliner.

Nov 27 Before the *Knowledge System* can finish asking, "Where is the washroom?" its user's manual has already opened itself to a page into which a bottomless hole has been cut. Whole epochs fall into it, never to be seen again.

Nov 30 "No," she rebutted emphatically at dinner last night, "the exiting stool does not approximate a second penis." We finished in silence her delicious baba ganoush.

Dec 1   The head of a wood louse, magnified a thousand times.

Dec 3   Abyssal stones.

Dec 4   Such loneliness this morning as I don't think I've ever experienced before, shitting out my substance as if in preparation for an embalming. Do the tiny insignificant agonies of my metabolism contribute to the texture or granularity of some supra-individual experience? Please? Or are they nothing more than brief flarings out from an oceanic and sovereign oblivion? Sieving shit by the seashore, then gone.

Dec 5   Kitchen sink–style defenestration through the judas window this morning. Such a bleak assortment of loose slab and palings and rookeries of meaningless shapes. I'm just a lonely unpaid stenographer for my refuse.

Dec 6   Why do I insist on trying to equate defecation with a speech act when I know full well there's no equation to be made? Is it just empty self-provocation? No, go deeper. There must be at work in this displacement the prohibition to take it in hand — my shit, I mean. Against the absence of manipulation (in the literal sense of word) I leverage a hackneyed deferral of signs.

Dec 7   Proscription as ground of consciousness. *I am not this* predates *I am*. Shit the primordial "not this."

Dec 12   Cromlechs and temples too are a perishable architecture.

Dec 13   "My blazonry is modest, for I have nothing to gain nor fear."

Dec 15   Soft diffident lumber.

Dec 18   Attempted once again last night at dinner to broach my speculations re: the "adjacency" of speaking and shitting. She dropped her fork and stormed off onto the patio. Watched her for the longest time, standing there facing the backyard with her arms crossed. The small panes of the French doors segmented her form in such a way that, for a split second, thought I recognized in one part of her head and right shoulder, segregated by the grid of panes from the rest of her body, the shape of some recent stool.

NOTE:

In 2008, the author was compelled, for reasons articulated to him by his gastroenterologist, to conduct the foregoing daily examinations for the duration of a year. When asked why it was necessary that the investigations be so protracted, the physician in question replied, somewhat cryptically, "All the rivers run into the sea, yet the sea is not full." By this the author took him to mean that other than mere physical benefits would accrue from a thorough notation of the work of his bowel.

THE TASK OF THE TRANSLATOR

THE TASK OF THE TRANSLATOR

THE TASK OF THE TRANSLATOR

THE TASK OF THE TRANSLATOR

WAYNE KOESTENBAUM

FALL 2003

Daisy was a poet; Gavin, a translator; Wayne, a teacher.

Gavin translated Daisy's poems, poorly, into English.

Wayne taught the inaccurate translations' deeply creased interstices.

Sometimes Gavin added meanings of his own.

Wayne taught these supplemental innuendos.

Daisy and Gavin were too young to remember the previous war.

Wayne invited Daisy and Gavin to visit his seminar and discuss translation's perils.

Daisy had an accident in the seminar. She broke down crying. Gavin tried to comfort her. Wayne vowed never again to teach Daisy's cloudy originals.

※

Gavin and Daisy had an affair.

Wayne changed his mind. He invited Daisy back to the seminar, despite her breakdown.

The seminar took place in a dungeon. Troublemaker Daisy read her originals into a distorting, crackly amplification system, which made the words more desirable.

※

Gavin made great money, translating Daisy, a star of underground cinema.

Wayne made a decent living, teaching Gavin's translations. Secretly Wayne wanted a direct erotic friendship with Daisy, but he settled for Gavin.

Wayne and Gavin always met for beers before class, so they could talk about Daisy's opacities.

Daisy was the genius, Gavin the conversationalist.

Gavin tried to translate breakdown. He grew exaggerated sideburns and wore tinted glasses. Daisy wore hippie skirts. Wayne taught the skirts and the translations, the originals and the sideburns.

※

Despite his relative affluence, Gavin lived at the Y. Daisy lived at the Waldorf.

Daisy thought her originals were flameproof so she set fire to them in her ice bucket. A bellboy put out the flame. Daisy faxed the charred fragments to Gavin, who translated them. Wayne taught the remains. Daisy's finger felt the wound.

※

Wayne took Daisy out for a drink. Gavin came along, to translate. Only Gavin could master Daisy's demanding multiplicity of dialects. The three friends ordered a plate of clattering mussels.

"Teach my originals," said Daisy, to Wayne, who shot Gavin a complicit look.

"You're a genius but I value my life," Wayne told Daisy.

"My loss is untranslatable," said Daisy, through Gavin. "And my finger hurts."

※

Then everything changed. Gavin discovered his voice. Daisy lost hers. Gavin became an original, and Daisy translated him.

Meanwhile, Wayne taught himself the rudiments of Daisy's language, a newfangled combination of several dispersed tongues.

Before class, Wayne and Daisy went out for beers to discuss Gavin's originals. Gavin wanted to come along, but Gavin, now that he was an original, had become untrustworthy, unsavory. As Wayne enveloped himself in Daisy's hippie skirts, the notion of the uncapturable trace came alive for him as never before.

※

Daisy and Gavin resumed their affair and videotaped themselves having sex. Wayne watched the videos. A bloody mess. Attractive. For sale. Dispersed remains. Daisy got her

voice back and Gavin lost his. Gavin returned to translation, and Daisy, to originality. Militant divisions. Everything returned to normal.

✕

Daisy wrote a poem about the imminent war. Gavin refused to translate it. He said it violated her contract. War changes the contract, Daisy argued. Gavin took off his shorts.

✕

Daisy had Biblical patches. Gavin's duty was to seek out the patches and remedy them, disguise their purple.

In their sex videos, Gavin and Daisy nude-wrestled, their bodies slick with the infantile.

Daisy and Gavin were still in their twenties. Their work had hardly begun. It was a pity that one of them would soon die.

✕

Daisy sounded like Ponge, Hikmet, and Tsvetaeva, but Gavin distorted her in translation, turning her into a bargain-basement Verlaine. He infelicitously translated Daisy's famous poem about a pebble. Wayne caught the errors but didn't dare tell Daisy that translation had soiled her pebble original.

✕

Against advice, Wayne showed his students the video of Gavin and Daisy nude-wrestling. Assignment: write a paragraph adjudicating the fight. The students en masse said they hated allegory. They refused to write the paragraphs. The twentieth century ended. The war began. Wayne wrote a paragraph. He brought his allegory to the bar and discussed it with Gavin, before class, while they drank beers. Gavin's alcoholism got worse, almost rising to Daisy's level.

✕

Daisy decided to take a shower before she wrote another poem about a pebble. She shampooed with Herbal Essence. Gavin joined her in the shower, put conditioner in her hair.

82

Wayne opened the bathroom door. "Can I come in?" he asked. Gavin said yes. Daisy said, "Please don't use your video camera." Gavin refused to translate. Wayne had forgotten his rudimentary knowledge of Daisy's vernacular. "Gavin," said Wayne, "do you mind if I video?" "That's fine," said Gavin." "I'm sick," said Daisy, "of Wayne's feeble literalism."

✕

And here are Daisy and Gavin, at the Oscars!

Daisy was nominated for best foreign original, and Gavin was nominated for best translation of a foreign original.

The winners are — Glenn Close opened the envelope — Daisy and Gavin! The theme music of the Daisy and Gavin movie began to play, and Daisy and Gavin walked onstage together to accept their Oscar, a Siamese twin statuette, joined at the ribcage. Afterward, downtown, Daisy and Gavin found a practitioner to bisect (illegal operation) the monstrous Oscar.

✕

Gavin got a lot of translation work for high prices because he was exceptionally handsome. Daisy's pebble poems were highly praised because she was very beautiful. Gavin got sexier, after the Oscar. Daisy got dumpy. Now Daisy was jealous of Gavin, his face on the covers of magazines. The translator and his sideburns. The translator and his room at the Y. A curious nation's shifting population watched Daisy and Gavin vie.

✕

Then Wayne and Gavin started having an affair, and Wayne checked into the Y, to be closer to Gavin. After sex, Wayne and Gavin went to the coffee shop across from the Y, to discuss Daisy's originals. Gavin's body got better and better, the longer the affair lasted.

Daisy continued to write further installments of her pebble poem. Gavin, at the coffee shop across from the Y, discussed the new translations with Wayne. Tonight Wayne was teaching the seven hundredth poem about the pebble, and Gavin couldn't explain a few of the nuances. "If I don't understand the pebble, Gavin, I can't teach this poem," Wayne said, exasperated, as he ate his hamburger and drank his malted milk. "We go about the

tasks of daily life," said Gavin, "in our own ways."

"Your translation is more confusing than the original," said Wayne.

Shocked, Gavin gripped the edge of the table. He froze and fell backward in time to a moment before he'd begun to translate.

※

Daisy's new project was a revision of Fernando Pessoa's *The Book of Disquiet*. Daisy called her version, *The Book of Perpetual Quiet*. Gavin had already begun to translate it, though Daisy had not finished writing it. Gavin worried that Daisy was not composing quickly enough. Wayne worried that Gavin was not translating quickly enough. Over beers, Gavin told Wayne that Daisy's *Book of Perpetual Quiet* was her most difficult work and the most exasperating to translate. Wayne replied that the task of the translator was to stop complaining. To escape the day's cruxes, the teacher reached his hand in the translator's pants.

※

"Every act of speech is site-specific," said Gavin, to Daisy. Wayne was filming their conversation with his video camera, so he could replay the event to his class. Wayne worried that Daisy's and Gavin's nudity would offend students.

The students were not offended. They applauded Daisy's and Gavin's bodies.

"In Daisy's pebble poems," said Wayne, to his seminar, "she is totally 'out there.'" Gavin, sitting in on the seminar, interrupted. "I disagree. In my translations of the pebble poem, I show that Daisy is completely grounded. That's the point of the pebble: to demonstrate Daisy's connection to diurnal things." Daisy was sitting at the other end of the conference table. She wore a pink wig today. She still had a wound on her right index finger, from the Waldorf ice bucket flame. Despite discomfort, Daisy took notes. Her new fluency in English surprised everyone. She was outgrowing the need for a translator. This fact upset her. She had more clout in the literary community if she relied on a translator. Originals were respected only if they passed through translation's veils. "I miss my power," Daisy whispered to herself, in the seminar. As she contemplated her vanishing clout, she began to cry. Georgie, a student who had a crush on Gavin and was doing a video documentary about Gavin's face,

began to film Daisy crying. Any exploitative footage was fodder. "I'm pissed," whispered Daisy, as Georgie filmed. "I'm pissed that the teacher doesn't get my pebble nuances."

✕

The task of the teacher is to translate.
The task of the translator is to wake up Daisy.
Daisy's pebble nuance poem is the translation of the burn.
The translator is the task of Daisy.
Gavin is the Daisy of Wayne.
The Waldorf is the translation of the Y.
The Y is the Waldorf of the translator.
The burn is the nuance of the pebble.
The task is the dispersal of the translator.
Gavin is the Oscar of the pebble nuance poem.
The seminar is the task of the burn.
The breakdown is the Oscar of the task.
The sexual fantasy is the task of the Y.
The breakdown of the translator is the task.
The seminar is the sexual fantasy of the translator.

✕

Multiple choice quiz:

1.) War is
   (a) the task of the translator
   (b) outside the story
   (c) the story
   (d) untranslatable
   (e) all of the above

2.) The task is
   (a) the translator
   (b) Daisy and Gavin's sexual incompatibility
   (c) Daisy's sexual voraciousness
   (d) Gavin's sexual hangups
   (e) how we got here and how we get out of here

3.) Shame is the tint of
    (a) the translator
    (b) the task
    (c) Daisy
    (d) the pebble nuance poem
    (e) untranslatability

※

Spleen
    a new poem by Daisy, translated by Gavin

Daisy, grand flotation device,
loves the pale inhabitants of the nearby cemetery
that pours its mortality on the smoky suburbs.

Daisy on the roadside looks for her litter
agitated without rest by the meager galette
that Gavin fed me when I tried to strangle his gullet
with my sad voice, all frill and phantom.

My pebble burden is perpetual mouth, lamentation
faucet that never turns off,
rheumatic dependency, foul ball, perfumed yard-sale.

Heritage is fatal, said Gavin, in the Waldorf,
under a hydroponic umbrella. The handsome valet
offered to undo my pique by sinisterly causing

my translatability to go falsetto.

※

In the dungeon, Wayne taught Gavin's translation of Daisy's "Spleen." Daisy attended the seminar. Her burn filled the room. The war began. Would we win was not the question. The question was how to translate the pronoun *we*.

※

"I don't want merely to fall back on rhetoric," Daisy said, to the seminar, on the second evening of the war. *Daisy's voice is newly transparent in the evening*, thought Gavin, afraid of being erased by

86

evening. Wayne was trying to teach the students about Gavin's fear of erasure and about Daisy's new transparency on the second evening of the war. "Tasks can't go on as usual," said Daisy to the room, but the room didn't trust her, because she was having another florid breakdown, carefully documented in the pebble nuance poem. Gavin was taking notes for a future translation of Daisy's in-class breakdown on the second evening of the war. Wayne was trying to teach Gavin's future notes, even before they were written down or translated, and this precipitousness, this earliness, was posing problems, complications to be discussed between teacher and translator, later, at the Y, in Gavin's room, after Daisy had returned to the Waldorf.

✕

Scarlatti wrote 600 sonatas, Daisy wrote in a poem that Gavin was trying to translate and that Wayne was trying to teach even before it had been translated; *Scarlatti wrote over 600 sonatas, and at his death,* wrote Daisy, in a poem that expanded on the work of the pebble nuance poem, *Scarlatti's manuscripts were dispersed, and his reputation fell into obscurity.* Gavin translated the lines poorly, but Wayne could see through the inadequate wording and in any case no longer taught translations, only originals. In the seminar, Gavin applied a bandage to Daisy's burned finger. In wartime it was only possible to teach originals, but no one in the seminar, including the teacher, fully understood Daisy's amalgam of tongues, or the sources of her wounds, or if her losses had origins.

✕

Ars Poetica
    a new poem by Daisy, translated by Gavin

Music comes first.
I prefer impairment.
The vaguer and airier, the better.
Less pizzicato, more posing.

It's also necessary to wander from the point
and to choose your words contemptuously
so you don't end up behaving like a grisette
in a Precision joint near the indecisive Rhine.

O beautiful derrière of Gavin, translating me!
O beautiful trembling day, nearly noon,
above autumn's accidents, the Kremlin
framing Daisy's love for Gavin's oyster-clear eyes!

Voilà, nuance, come, again and again,
into my pebble poem, colored red or yellow
according to my fiancé's whim —
I hop from dream to dream like a flute having a coronary

and I try to assassinate —
good Daisy that I am — every impure thought,
every "point," every cruel azure argument —

you can take your elegance, Gavin,
and shove it up your ass! feral
Being, assuaged by rhyme,
veiled by the Almost, the Nearly —

I'll sue you, rather than step
forged into the lime-bright falseness of this age,

musical as the Aga Khan though no one cares,
enveloped by agency
and within the alleys of your decisiveness
arguing a footpath between brother and other.

Good luck, Gavin,
I'm parsing you as best I can.
The bed you sleep in isn't literature's.

✖

Next year, Gavin and Daisy were nominated for Oscars
again — Daisy, for best foreign original, and Gavin, for best
translation of a foreign original. Daisy lost. Gavin won. Gavin
had carefully crafted an acceptance speech, which he read aloud
to the gathered crowd. After reading it, onstage, he shot himself
in the heart. Daisy, in the audience, ran up to him and threw
her living body over his dead one. The next week, Wayne taught
Gavin's acceptance speech in his translation seminar. Here is the
speech in its entirety:

Translation, like triumph, is a subject I can approach only cautiously.

If I had a language other than my own, perhaps I could broach this subject, and this imperial occasion, with more fortitude and clarity; in the absence of a substitute language, I must regard this subject as one too daunting to trifle with, too large to avoid. Lucky indeed am I to be in the position of speaking to you today about this matter, a matter I shall call the opposite of weightless, a matter unapproachable despite my surprising victory; for today's occasion, untranslatable, proposes a subject before which any thinking and feeling woman or man, any woman or man with a sense of historical consequence, must tremble; a subject before which we must take unusual pains, lest we damage ourselves or our listeners by mishandling a single nuance of the burden I would not call "word-hauntedness" if there were a better noun in my forlorn and bewildered language to describe the task.

CONTEMPORARY BALLETS

FROM *1001* CONCISE
CONTEMPORARY BALLETS

FROM *1001* CONCISE
CONTEMPORARY BALLETS

FROM *1001* CONCISE
CONTEMPORARY BALLETS

RICHARD KOSTELANETZ

FALL 2000

A good libretto, even an impressionist, double-exposed or portmanteaued one, follows most of the rules of simple dramaturgy. Balanchine once said the perfect type plot for a dramatic narrative ballet was the story of the Prodigal Son. Once there was a man who had everything, then he had nothing; finally he had everything again.
— Lincoln Kirstein
Ballet Alphabet (1939)

Two impresarios try to steal each other's dancers, in full view of each other.

Among the guests at a party honoring a prima ballerina is a young man who falls in love with her and she with him; but as she recalls former lovers, who dress to resemble one another, she realizes that not only is this new suitor beneath her standards but that of loving men she has simply had enough.

Inspired by birdlike movements, this ballet is essentially pilotless.

The girls of a port town find the ship captain so irresistible that they disguise themselves as beardless young sailors to board his ship, where they discover, as he makes advances on them, that the captain must be essentially homosexual.

Two prisoners escape to the home of one whose wife falls in love with the other, who is persuaded to kill her husband but then, under the persistent threat of arrest, he remains hidden in her house, eventually realizing that he has simply exchanged one prison for another, the new one only slightly less disagreeable than its predecessor.

Several performers, as naked as acceptable, smear one another

with chocolate syrup whose smell becomes so overwhelming that chocolate-hungry members of the audience on their own initiative come on stage to lick spatulas and even the performers' bodies. (Their needs should not be spurred.)

A man with an easily divisible personality is torn severely between body and soul, convention and dissidence, wealth and love; his role can be played by two or more dancers.

The assassins who appear to be male turn out to be women.

Though from all appearances she looked like a contemporary woman, the prima donna was also a skilled automotive mechanic.

An athletic woman who tries repeatedly to do four jetés in mid-air finally succeeds, disappearing above the proscenium.

In an all-night performance, several dancers represent the planets slowly rotating around the sun, whose role is played by the choreographer.

Thanks to effects possible with videotape, we see on the small screen a man, obviously exhausted, continually climbing upward to heaven and repeatedly passing a sign marked only with an infinity symbol.

On the white classic leotards of scores of dancers are projected both radical contemporary political slogans and abstract lines resembling the tread marks of radical tires.

All available spotlights are shined directly at the audience, preferably in steadily increasing numbers, until everyone leaves.

A prostitute enslaved by a demonic pimp is required to murder her customers until she encounters a man who, even though he is stabbed many times, does not die.

In a black mass, with three archangels presiding, a young woman makes a Faustian wager, transforming herself, thanks to angelic hocus-pocus, into the contemporary embodiment of excessive knowledge — a hard computer disc that lies under a spotlight at the center of the stage.

The protagonist is someone, apparently a dance patron, for whom everyone is continually waiting, even though he or she doesn't appear.

In a ballet accompanied by primitive music, a devilish young woman, dancing with extravagant movements, strangles prospective suitors with her extended ponytail.

During an hour of continuous movement, a game of musical chairs evolves into a brawl that requires the intervention of the police.

The protagonist falls into an epileptic fit when her father tells her to marry someone other than the man she loves, and she has even more extravagant fits when her father offers yet other suitors.

According to the program, "The purpose of this ballet is to represent male-female relationships realistically — as harmonious as they should be."

Before any human performers appear, water floods onto the stage and out into the audience, which is forced to leave. Their commotion becomes the ballet.

Before a projection of a bombed-out city, the dancers construct a tent from urban scrap.

In this version of *Alice in Wonderland*, all the dancers working in a studio conspire to crash into a mirror that, when it breaks, becomes a doorway to another world.

Christ is reborn in an urban slum, experiencing again, after a period of miraculous good deeds, a crucifixion and resurrection whose significance is apparent not to those around him but to the audience.

OF THE MINE VERSUS THE MIND
AND THE HARVARD OUTLINE

OUTLINE TOWARDS A THEORY
OF THE MINE VERSUS THE MIND
AND THE HARVARD OUTLINE

OUTLINE TOWARDS A THEORY
OF THE MINE VERSUS THE MIND
AND THE HARVARD OUTLINE

ANDER MONSON

SPRING 2004

I. Start with the roman numeral I with an authoritative period trailing just after it. This is the Harvard Outline, which comes In Caps, and is a method of organizing information
    a. remembered from high school as a major step towards creating an essay
        i. though there was a decimal method, too
    b. but I've never been comfortable with the thing — its seeming rigor, its scaffolding so white against the language
        i. never felt the top-down structuralist method of constructing writing to be useful or effective; the mind, so idiosyncratic, unusual
            1. its strangeness and its often-incoherence
                a. the lovely anomaly
    c. and The Harvard Outline is the reason that I get 55 five-paragraph essays every month
    d. it is, I think, suspect (its
    e. headings
        i. subheadings
            1. sub-subheadings
                a. etc.
                b. though there is a pleasure to this iteration, this recursion — like mathematics and the algorithms I played with and admired in computer science classes, writing functions that called themselves
                    i. which called themselves
                        1. which called themselves
                            a. until they were satisfied
                        2. and exited

      ii. right back
   c. out
       i. like those Russian nesting
        (matryoshka) dolls; a lovely
        symmetry; such satisfaction
        comes in nesting
      ii. such starkness
        1. elegance),
 f. all those steps out and down across the page — like the
  writing task is that of going downhill, like a waterfall in its
  rush
    i. or the incremental, slow plod down the slope, skis
    buried behind in some drift
 g. While technically called "The Harvard Outline"
    i. it has nothing to do with Harvard
      1. according to their archivists, "it appears to be
      a generic term"
    ii. so it's difficult to track it down in the history of
    organizing information
      1. which is what this culture spends increasing
      time (and money!) doing
        a. witness the amazing success of the
        search-engine Google
          i. as created by Larry Page and
          Sergey Brin
          ii. with its elegant mechanism of
          concordance
            1. of ranking searches by
            the number of pages that
            link to each individual
            page or site in order to
            establish the relative
            importance of that initial
            page or site
              a. and look —
              there's no need
              for parentheses in
              1. above thanks
              to the Harvard
              Outline
              b. again that
              attraction to self-
              examination

      c. again that
        attraction to
        what elegance
        there is to find

II. My family has a background in the Michigan mining industry
- a. a history in copper, iron, the cast-off leftover materials necessary to process ore from rock
- b. though less my recent family
  - i. not my father who is a professor — whose job, like mine, is the mining and refining, then the distribution of information for (small sums of) money
    1. though perhaps this is a cynical view of the profession
       - a. and light as knowledge metaphor is hardly breaking new ground
    2. still I like the image of the light-helmeted professor plowing through the darkness
       - a. though it is romantic to say the least
    3. "like mine" (from above) — mining is a story of possession
       - a. of legal ownership of land and rights, the permission to go below the crust
    4. "breaking new ground" (from above) — again the construction terminology
       - a. the invocation of the building, of the engineering
    5. my father teaches at Michigan Technological University, formerly the Michigan College of Mines, a school that is just about to lose its Mining Engineering program
       - a. which is older than the oldest living humans
       - b. which is "one of only 15 mining engineering programs in the U.S. that has been uninterrupted since the beginning of the century and has also held accreditation with the Accreditation Board for Engineering and Technology (ABET) since 1936," according to the MTU Mining Engineering website
         - i. this tidbit brought to you

through Google
ii. this tidbit being no longer accurate (now we should use past tense, as the program has been retired, killed, phased out): this is an information shift between the writing of the essay and its publication

c. but further back
    i. since nearly everyone who emigrated to Upper Michigan from (mostly) Scandinavia worked in the mines, or worked in industries that supported it
        1. the mining boom in the 19th century was so big that Calumet, Michigan, population of 879 as of the 2000 census, was nearly named the capitol of Michigan
        2. and there are stories of exploitation and immense hardship
            a. as there always are
        3. though just after WWII, the price of copper declined and so — though there's still plenty underneath the Northern earth — the mines slowly shut their doors
            a. now there are no active producing mines left in the Keweenaw,
                i. the railroads no longer run
                ii. even the Greyhound bus service has stopped
                iii. it felt at times while growing up like living in a dead letter office
                    1. another information shift: evidently there are still two mines that remain in operation, one of my which my high school friend Jeremy, his father a metallurgist, is working for
            b. though the shells they left behind — the fine network of tunnels that still riddle the earth — are havens for millions of bats
                i. who come out at night through

   the chicken wire that often
   covers up the mines' mouths
  ii. and were — until recently,
   when the method of closing off
   the mines was changed to be a
   bit more bat-friendly — picked
   off by hundreds of raccoons that
   would sit at the chicken wire,
   waiting for the daily exodus and
   feast
 c. and now Upper Michigan is a
  destination for bat-watching tourists
d. and anyone growing up in the Keweenaw has had ready
 access to mines
  i. either through the tours of the few remaining open
   tourist mines
   1. which are absolutely worth doing, though
    expensive (to the tune of $25), because to be
    submerged a mile underneath the earth is a
    necessary experience
    a. to get that absolute darkness
     i. even if you think you know
      what it's like
    b. and to get that absolute *chill*
    c. to know what your ancestors went
     through
     i. or at least to have an idea — isn't
      this an honor or an obligation?
  ii. or more likely illegally
   1. breaking the locks off the doors
    a. because there are hundreds of old
     shafts sunk in the land that haven't
     been filled
   2. drinking inside (also arguably a family
    obligation), or exploring with rope, flashlights,
    and a constant sense of possibility
    a. for there is something beautiful, nearly
     unbearable, about a hole in the earth
     i. about darkness
      1. that unknown
       a. black box
        i. big X
     ii. maybe it's a male fixation

b. that it must bear exploration, no matter how far down it goes

    i. maybe it's too many Hardy Boys books, or Jules Verne

c. and also there's the danger

    i. a definite attraction

        1. one cure for boredom

        2. a cheapie dangerous carnival ride

iii. or possibly through the few research mines maintained by the university

    1. one of which I discovered while hiking in Hancock, Michigan

        a. while it's not a public mine, it is not gated or barred off

        b. walk within a quarter of a mile and you'll feel the drop in temperature caused by the cool air streaming out

            i. a counterintuitive finding — remember high school geology, the earth's crust, mantle, core, etc., and lava bursting out through craters

            ii. or Jules Verne again

                1. while less than absolutely reliable

            iii. and how it gets hotter now

                1. the farther

                    a. in

                        i. you go

            iv. how there's a sort of pressure from the outside structure

                1. how the structure

                    a. either binds you in or wants to expel you like a sickness

                    b. think the mine, the outline, as a body

                    c. an ecosystem

                    d. or a mechanical spring

                    i. compress
                    ii. release
                    iii. repeat
            v. and that structure creates
                pressure; how architecture is the
                elegant distribution of stress

III. The outline, so like a mine
    e. defined by penetration
        i. deeper in
        ii. both laterally and vertically
            1. for harder information
        iii. yes, how male, again, you dirty bird
    f. Mining is interested mostly in the horizontal
        i. mineral deposits — in the absence of fault or other
            geologic strangeness — lay naturally in planes
        ii. since similar materials respond similarly to pressure,
            they settle horizontally
        iii. and the goal of the miner is to identify the deposit
            1. in terms of *dip and strike*
                a. the straight line of maximum
                    inclination (*dip*)
                b. the horizontal line, the contour line
                    (*strike*)
    g. and the vertical when necessary, to either follow the vein
        i. or to proceed deeper into the earth once the vein has
            been exhausted
    h. though the terminology of the mine is far more lovely than of
        the outline
        i. *level, incline, drifs, shaft, crosscut, winze, raise and mouth and
            face, gossan, apex, shaft, adit, gangue, stope*
        ii. *"Shallow Boring in Soft Rocks: Boring by Hand Auger"*
            1. chapter subheading from the "Boring"
                chapter, *Introduction to Mining* by Bohuslav
                Stoces
        iii. having an essential mystery to them
            1. due to their inaccessibility
                a. compare to that of the Harvard
                    Outline, designed particularly (one
                    imagines — though it's not clear who
                    designed it) to be easily negotiable
            2. and the aura of danger, of esoteric, academic,
                secret knowledge about them
                a. they literally describe loci of danger,

pits and sinkholes; they offer both
treasure and death
    i. both of which have a lure
iv. and I was obsessed with mining for the first ten years
of my life
    1. visiting the A. E. Seaman Mineralogical
Museum at Michigan Technological
University
        a. which has the 17-ton copper boulder,
the largest mineral specimen ever taken
from Lake Superior
        b. an emblem of the Keweenaw, one of
the world's richest copper deposits
    2. trying to convince my dad to buy me various
geological supplies
        a. such as the rock tumbler I never really
used — a sad emblem of my childhood
sitting on a shelf maybe in my parents'
basement
    3. agate hunting along the shores of Lake
Superior
    4. looking for chunks of unrefined copper in
the woods or in the hills of stamps and along
Portage Canal (the canal that cuts off the tip
of the Keweenaw Peninsula from Michigan)
        a. leftovers from processing iron ore
        b. that very well may be poisoning some
Michigan lakes
            i. and we try not to think too
much about this
    5. making homemade explosives according to
the often-poor instructions from Paladin Press
books and other, even less reliable sources
        a. ceasing only when a good friend of
mine lost three fingers
v. and in a way, I still am — as it's the central story of
the place where I am from, the big goodness and the
tragedy
    1. it is how I imagine the ghost of slavery is to
Southern writers
        a. having this central, public history
contributes to there even being such a
thing as a "Southern Writer," whereas

there aren't as obviously "Northern Writers"

    2. (the boom and the bust — the makings of story itself)

        a. and certainly the makings of much of my family

i. perhaps it's only my desire

    i. that this, my kind of work

        1. darkness on light onscreen, then on the page

    ii. be worth as much as what my family did in the dark for hours

j. and the metaphor of mining one's past or childhood for writing material

    i. an apt construction, experience as *material*

    ii. is used a lot, and is something I'm concerned about myself

        1. the ethics and the economics of the writing act

            a. and that other pressure that it entails

                i. so maybe the outline is a kind of architecture I am trying to erect

                ii. to protect myself against my family, meaninglessness, and the future

                    1. an artifice to get inside the past

                    2. like a cold and unlit hole — what family tragedy is there behind me glittering like a vein

                iii. perhaps it is a womb

                    1. and this then has to do with my mother's death

                    2. a protective sheath, a comfort zone

                iv. or it could be a shell

            b. an attempt for rigor as some buffer or protection

            c. or maybe it is elegance for the sake of it

            d. an infinite recursion

            e. some wankery

    2. then there's always the possibility of being stuck, candle snuffed by a sudden blast

        a. the candles that my family would have

to buy themselves and carry — lit —
down into the earth, the candles that
were the only protection against the
emptiness and isolation
3. with no way of lighting up again, and no way
iii. back out —

MONUMENT

MONUMENT

MONUMENT

MONUMENT

MONUMENT

MARY RUEFLE

FALL 2001

A small war had ended. Like all wars, it was terrible. Things which had stood in existence were now vanished. I had come back because I had survived and survivors come back, there is nothing else left for them to do. I had been on long travels connected to the war, and I had been to the centerpiece of the war, that acre of conflagration. And now I was sitting on a park bench, watching ducks land and take off from a pond. They too had survived, though I had no way of knowing if they were the same ducks from before the war or if they were the offspring of ducks who had died in the war. It was a warm day in the capital and people were walking without coats, dazed by the warmth, which was not the heat of war, which had engulfed them, but the warmth of expansion, in which would grow the idea of a memorial to the war, which had ended, and of which I was a veteran architect. In knew I would be called upon for my ideas in regard to this memorial and I had entered the park aimlessly, trying to escape my ideas, as I had been to the centerpiece, that acre of conflagration, and from there the only skill that returned was escapement, and others died with those who possessed them. I was dining with friends that evening, for the restaurants and theaters and shops had reopened, the capital was like a great table cloth being shaken in midair so that life could be smoothed and reset and go on, and I had in my mind a longing to eat, and to afterward order my favorite dessert, cherries jubilee, which would be made to flame and set in the center of the table, and I had in my mind the idea of submitting to the committee a drawing of an enormous plate of cherries, perpetually burning, to be set in the center of the park, as a memorial to the war, that acre of conflagration. And perhaps also in my mind was the hope that such a ridiculous idea would of course be ignored and as a result I would be left in peace, the one thing I desired, even beyond cherries. And I could see the committee, after abandoning my idea, remaining in their seats fighting over the designs of others,

far into the after-hours of the workday, their struggles never seeming to end, and then I wanted to submit an idea of themselves as a memorial for the war, the conference table on an island in the middle of the pond, though at least some of them would have to be willing to die in the enactment. And then I saw on the ground an unnamed insect in its solitary existence, making its laborious way through tough blades of grass that threatened its route, and using a stick that lay nearby I drew a circle around the animal — if you can call him that — and at once what had been but a moment of middling drama became a theater of conflict, for as the insect continued to fumble lopsided in circles it seemed to me that his efforts had increased, not only by my interest in them, but by the addition of a perimeter of which he now seemed intent on escaping. I looked up then, and what happened next I cannot describe without a considerable loss of words: I saw a drinking fountain. It had not suddenly appeared, it must have always been there, it must have been there as I walked past it and sat down on the bench, it must have been there yesterday, and during the war, and in the afternoons before the war. It was a plain gunmetal drinking fountain, of the old sort, basin on a pedestal, and it stood there, an ordinary object that had become an unspeakable gift, a wonder of civilization, and I had an overwhelming desire to see if it worked, I stood up then and approached it timidly, as I would a woman, I bent low and put my hand on its handle and my mouth hovered over its spigot — I wanted to kiss it, I was going to kiss it — and I remembered with a horrible shock that in rising from the bench I had stepped on and killed the insect, I could hear again its death under my left foot, though this did not deter me from finishing my kiss, and as the water came forth with a low bubbling arch first and finally an arch that reached my mouth, I began to devise a secret route out of the park that would keep me occupied for some time, when I looked up, holding miraculous water in my mouth, and saw the ducks in midflight, their wings shedding water drops which returned to the pond, and remembered in amazement that I could swallow, and I did, then a bit of arcane knowledge returned to me from an idle moment of reading spent years ago, before the war; that a speculum is not only an instrument regarded by most with horror, as well as an ancient mirror, and a medieval compendium of all knowledge, but a patch of color on the lower wing segments of most ducks and some other birds. Thus I was able, in serenest peace, to make my way back to my garret and design the memorial which was not elected and never built, but remained for me an end to the war that had ended.

BODILY VIOLENCE AS
SEEN IN REACTION
TO STRESS IN ADOLESCENTS

BODILY VIOLENCE AS
SEEN IN REACTION
TO STRESS IN ADOLESCENTS

BODILY VIOLENCE AS
SEEN IN REACTION
TO STRESS IN ADOLESCENTS

GENEVIEVE TURKETT

SPRING 2007

Introduction

"She was shaking so hard I was sure she would break," is just one of many descriptions provided to us by one Officer Winters of Precinct 32, as pertinent to our "Physical Effects" lab work. The purpose of this specific experiment, as commented on by Winters, was to observe the physical affects, specifically bodily violence, of witnessing a traumatic event upon ~~me~~ adolescent females. It was conducted within one day over the course of approximately one hour. No outside sources were used.

The general objective for this experiment was to understand ~~my~~ the human body's reaction to stress and the levels and progression of the biological responses in adolescents. Specifically, one ~~Gen~~ Phoebe Parker. The experiment was conducted within one part, inside the ~~Jef~~ Tarla County Courthouse. ~~It was raining that day, slightly and persistently on the long windows~~. The weather information and time of day were not pertinent. A friend of ~~mine~~ Miss Parker's, Mr. Michael Williams, was on trial for 2 counts of homicide in the second and third degree, and also for assault of Miss Parker ~~he didn't mean it~~ and numerous others ~~maybe he didn't mean it~~. For the purpose of this experiment we observed Miss Parker in the courthouse when the trial did not begin ~~it was just his growing up~~, as she walked to where Mr. Williams was being held, and her final reaction to the trauma provided. With all of these locations chosen and laid out before-hand, ~~it was unbearable~~ the experiment went as planned.

Materials and Methods

The subject, Miss Parker, entered the courthouse from the rear door and took her seat at the front of the room at the prosecution's table. A lawyer spoke to ~~me~~ her. ~~He made me~~

afraid. He seemed to have no effect on her composure. The judge entered with a particularly ~~grave~~ stern look on his face and announced in ~~a 3 minute speech that tore at my insides and made me want to vomit~~ a loud voice that the trial had been extended

Number of Police Officers Noticing Phobe after 17 Minutes

to March 15 ~~tell the whole truth and nothing but the truth~~ for Mr. William's immediate family. His head drooped then with expected news ~~he was just a kid~~ and that the case against Mr. Williams ~~Michael~~ had been ~~there's something he wasn't saying~~ dismissed. The lawyer then began to usher ~~don't push she told us in kindergarten~~ Miss Parker and the two other witnesses ~~something feels sick~~ out of the courtroom. At this point ~~I~~ Miss Parker's hands began shaking ~~those bars of light through the windows slashing at my fingers~~ and our observations began. The next 17 minutes were watched closely and calculated carefully. ~~No one even paid attention to me~~ Not a moment was missed.

I ran to the door where I saw Officer Winters walk out of that morning. I knew he was there. Assuming that Miss Parker had no previous knowledge of where ~~Michael~~ Mr. Williams was being held, we believe that she was trying desperately to find an exit. As we followed, we entered the holding cell behind the courtroom behind I knew something like this would happen Phoebe. Within the room we took note of her almost immediate crying. Her hands began to shake much less but her entire body began to convulse with enormous, painful sobs crying. At the sight of ~~Michael Michael~~ Mr. Williams hanging from the ~~ceiling beams ceiling beams ceiling beams burst blood vessels under the ceiling beams~~ her reaction was appropriate.

Her hands became steady as she grasped her elbows and began breathing heavily and vibrating throughout her ~~he was just a kid he didn't know~~ entire body. Reaching the halfway mark of about eight ~~hours days childhoods~~ minutes, we also added a new criteria to our "bodily violence," that being a nosebleed. ~~I gasped at the sight of my own blood~~ She took another deep breath when her nose began to bleed ~~Michael Michael never knew what cult meant~~ but she made no effort to wipe it from ~~my~~ her face. Her heavy wheezing began to subside ~~I couldn't breathe~~ and though she continued to cry ~~I was broken completely~~ she made virtually no noise ~~all I could hear were his feet clunking against the metal bars.~~

Worth mentioning here is that only one officer noticed ~~me~~ Phoebe in the room, until all of them noticed at the 17-minute mark, ending our observation. One such officer was an Officer Tandy ~~with large arms and rocky hands~~ who had grasped onto ~~my~~ Phoebe's shoulders. The officer said nothing to her but rather stood ~~with his mouth gaping~~ still behind her. The room was chaotic with officers running around in circles and making phone calls ~~that no one noticed the crying 15-year-old watching his feet clunking against the bars.~~ At this point Phoebe's nosebleed was steadily increasing as we reached the 14-minute mark and ~~I~~ she began walking toward the ~~my friend~~ cell. ~~Most people think you just have to stand on a chair and kick it out from under you but then you'll just suffocate you really have to jump really hard from something high like a sink in a jail cell and your eyes bleed~~ She reached through the bars and touched one of his ~~swinging~~ feet.

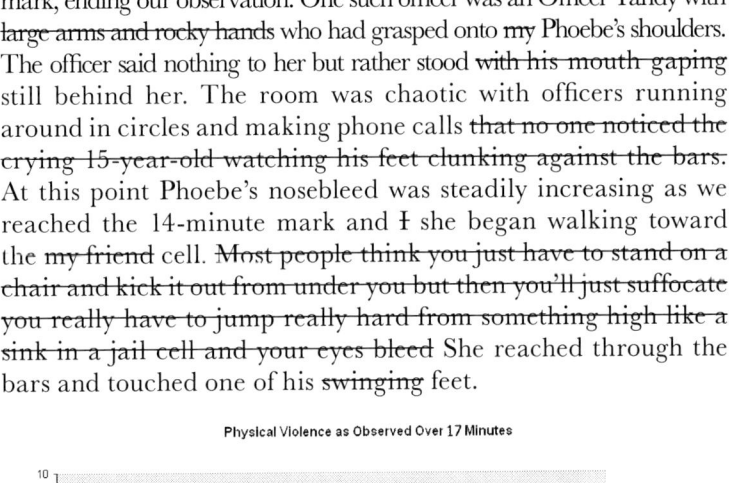

Physical Violence as Observed Over 17 Minutes

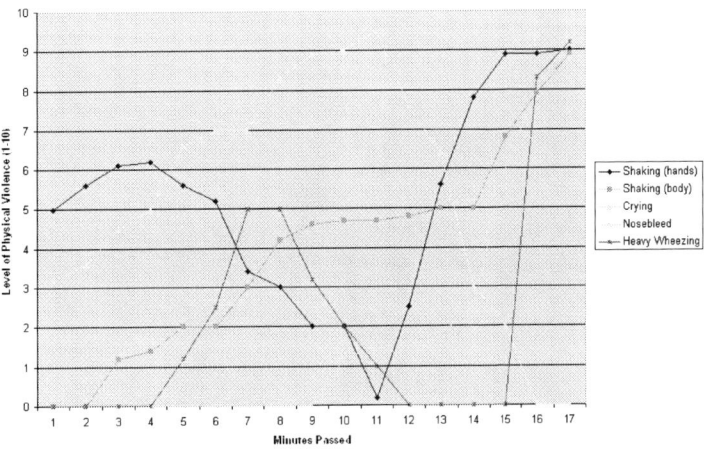

Here her breathing became ~~giant~~ gasps and her nose ~~burst~~ bled more profusely than it had yet. She began shaking violently. She let go of ~~my~~ her elbows and tried to grab the bars ~~to save him~~ but her hands shook too greatly to get a grip ~~blood all over~~. At the 16-minute mark nearly all of our criteria ~~pain~~ reached their top marks, except for crying which had ceased completely ~~your eyes bleed.~~ She ~~chanted~~ said his name ~~as if I was worshiping his drowned corpse~~ and still no officer noticed ~~my tiny crumbling body~~ her presence.

After 17 minutes the other three ~~creatures~~ officers in the room noticed ~~me~~ her falling to her knees ~~falling to my knees at the base of his cage. I could see the blood on the floor from his poor, bursting eyeballs. His head was cocked like he was so confused. He could see me I knew that he could see me but he just kept swinging back and forth slowlyslowlyslowly~~ and asking for forgiveness. The other three officers saw ~~me~~ her and scooped ~~me~~ her up ~~in their smulky arms to take me away from drowning~~ and removed her from the holding cell. Our observation ended and calculations were compiled after 17 minutes.

Possible sources of error ~~pain~~ could have been the ~~blood arms floor feet shoes~~ abnormal construction on the courthouse creating the holding cells ~~places to run where there was truth in judge's mouths~~, which created unusual ~~dragged away arms bruising on walls and bars~~ circumstances and possible skewing of results. Also, the police ~~bastards~~ could have been poorly trained, Miss Parker's friends ~~bastards~~ could have stayed in the room after Miss Parker ran into the holding area, and ~~I~~ Miss Parker herself choosing to ~~couldn't leave or run with my blood tying me like a rope to that sinking ugly thing~~ stay in the room rather than leave was highly unusual and created unexpected results. Overall we ~~tried I tried I knew he was a good good Michael friend~~ believe our observations were educational and productive ~~sad little feet in prison shoes knocking on the bars in singsong singsong like we sang~~ in the study of bodily violence ~~black eyes~~ as exhibited in adolescents when exposed ~~left to die~~ to severe trauma.

Discussion

~~I just see his sad neck stripped of skin on the right side with tiny specks on blood on his chin. He's got his eyebrows raised like he's laughing and his mouth lolls open. His poor, bleeding eyeballs staring at me and praying at me to let him~~

down. I'm yelling cut him down cut him down but no one hears me and some officer is yelling cut him down so he heard me and his big smulky arms touch me. Michael Michael Michael Mr. Williams has got Phoebe watching him watching him while he swings like a baby in a little rope chair or a swing. His big hands are blue like they used to be on the monkey bars or bike handles when he said my family is weird and I played and listened and swung next to his big arms. Houses on streets with backyards full of bodies and he was just a kid and didn't know he didn't know and cults are cults and murder is murder and kids are kids and I never learned how to ride a bike and Michael's dead and dead is dead.

There will be no discussion portion.

CHICAGO RADIO

CHICAGO RADIO

CHICAGO RADIO

CHICAGO RADIO

CHICAGO RADIO

WENDY WALTERS

FALL 2006

Listening to music underwater affects one's hearing in curious ways. No visible change can be seen in the shape of the eardrum, but many report being able to hear whispers from people they have never met for days after coming to the surface. Investigations into this phenomenon have been labeled crackpot science and hoodoo though among astrologers and criminologists interest grows.

※

In 2005 more than a million black people lived in Chicago, IL, making it a good place to win friends and stop being a stranger.

Other predominantly black cities like St. Louis, MO, and Detroit, MI, had frequent sightings of UFOs.

※

CALLER: My name is Mimi, and I would like to dedicate a song for my dad.

DJ: Go ahead.

CALLER: Just start talking?

DJ: Just start talking.

CALLER: His name is Earl. The last time I saw him he was working as an electrician for Delta Airlines at O'Hare in 1995.

Dad, you can come home now, and please don't worry too much about the past. This song has no words because I don't want to make any more promises.

I still love you.

※

Geography and racial inequality work against even the most nutritionally conscious moms.

A study of 266 black women in Detroit found that those who shopped in supermarkets ate more servings of fruits and vegetables per day than those who shopped at independent neighborhood grocery stores.

One area of Detroit that was 97% African American had no chain supermarkets and twelve independent grocery stores.

A nearby mixed-race area had ten independent groceries and seven chain supermarkets.

※

New data about the connections between nutrition and violence is changing the way people think about prison. Oxford University scientist Bernard Gesch tracked 231 maximum-security inmates over twelve months, recording violent or antisocial incidents. He gave one group a vitamin supplement, while a control group got a placebo. Over the next several months he saw a 35% drop in fighting among the group receiving vitamin supplements.

※

CALLER: I would like you to play a song for my fiancé. I don't know which one, can you pick it?

DJ: Sure thing. Hey, how did he propose?

CALLER: It was pretty plain.

DJ: Oh yeah? What did he do?

CALLER: He said, *I want you to be my wife. Do you want to be my wife?*

DJ: That doesn't sound plain to me. When are you getting married?

CALLER: We don't know. He's overseas right now.

DJ: Fighting?

CALLER: Yeah.

※

Rather than suffer the indignities of slavery, hundreds of thousands of Africans chose to drown while crossing the Atlantic. Some DJs claim no one drowned at all and those who leapt from deck landed below the ocean on a subcontinent called Drexciya.

It can be hard to get a message through when people are underwater.

※

Police Officer Martin Farr described the evacuation of a Chicago public high school after the storm passed:

A woman, she was about the age of my mother, maybe fifty years or so, was standing at a podium in front of a large classroom. She spoke to her students in a stern tone of voice about personal responsibility. When I turned around to note their reaction, I realized the back half of the building had been blown away by the storm. Torn strips of corrugated steel hung over a gaping hole in which oily, brown water was rushing in. Soon it was up to our chests. The teacher seemed unmoved by the flood, but she was overcome with disappointment in her students' inability to call out their presence at attendance.

※

A glowing red object flew over a residential area of New Haven, CT, in November 1953, causing lights on both sides of the object's path to dim then come back on when it went out of sight. This signified the beginning of an increase in New Haven's black population.

In 1950, African Americans comprised only 12.25% of New

Haven's population. By 2000, New Haven was 43.5% white and 37.4% African-American.

✕

A plane filled with prisoners being transported to a federal facility in Wyoming took off from Chicago's O'Hare Airport in April. Ascending into low clouds over Lake Michigan, it disappeared from radar. The plane showed up several hours later over the Florida Keys, heading toward a tropical storm gathering force off the western coast of Cuba. For about thirty minutes Miami controllers tried to reestablish radio contact. When the plane vanished for the final time all the controllers involved in the search fell asleep and were unable to be wakened for one hour.

✕

DJ: Who am I talking to?

CALLER: This is James.

DJ: James, what can I do for you tonight?

CALLER: Could you play a song for my baby's mother? We're not getting along too good, and I just want her to know that I love her.

DJ: What's going on?

CALLER: Well, ever since our daughter was born she has been afraid to leave her with me because I am visually impaired.

DJ: Did she know you were visually impaired when you, you know, conceived your daughter?

CALLER: Yes.

DJ: And now she has an issue with that?

CALLER: Yes, well —

DJ: Do you think that she really has an issue with that or is she mad about something else?

CALLER: Uh —

DJ: Is there anything else that might be worrying her?

CALLER: I just want her to know that I plan on being a really good dad and that I love her, I love them both a lot.

DJ: I'm sorry you are having such a hard time, James, and I hope the two of you can work it out.

CALLER: Can you play a song for me?

DJ: Not right now.

※

This account comes from a former member of the Chicago Police Department now working as a security guard for a local supermarket chain.

A soldier recently returned from the war was teaching his eight-year-old brother combat techniques for a shoreline invasion. They dug a trench wide enough to hold them both and then enacted the kind of gestures they would perform in response to a heavy artillery attack. The younger brother grew bored with the exercise and pleaded to go home. The older brother, overcome with thoughts of war, sat down for a moment to collect himself. A sudden surge from the lake surprised him. He was knocked unconscious by the force of the wave and dragged under as his younger brother watched from the hill.

When the younger brother finally made his way home, he was unable to speak. I was called in to raise the elder brother from the dead so that the younger one might convey his regret in being unable to save him. We went back to the beach. Because the surf was still choppy from the recent storm, it was not difficult to conjure the spirit of the soldier. His face looked badly scratched and bruised. When he tried to talk, only sand and water came out of his mouth. The younger brother made his apology. The soldier accepted this apology begrudgingly because things had not turned out how he thought they would. He extended his hand to his young brother. That contact left a permanent scar on the boy's hand, a smooth, white patch in the shape of a "Y" that would itch whenever the boy became frightened.

※

For several summers in a cemetery on the city's South Side, a man grew turnips and mustard greens, spinach, callaloo, and rapini on the plot that would become his grave. Each crop had grown quite large. He claimed he fed himself for the entire winter on what he raised on his narrow field, but this year someone stole his harvest.

A police officer doubted they would find the perpetrator. The other officer handed the man a bag of groceries he had picked up for his family just before the call. Inside the bag there were canned peas and carrots, green beans, corn, and white potatoes.

※

DJ: Go ahead with your long-distance dedication.

CALLER: This song is for my grandmother, who taught me how to use coupons to shop around to get the best prices on groceries. She bought a green Pinto in 1970, and we used to go everywhere together.

DJ: You guys used to go out on little adventures, huh? Where did she take you?

CALLER: Well, we would start out at Food Town in Quakertown, PA, where we bought evaporated milk, biscuit mix, and canned sardines.

And then we would head to Zeller's in Windsor, ON, where we bought canned Jamaican ackee fruit for her next-door neighbors, Mr. and Mrs. MacDonald, who they said tasted like scrambled eggs.

At Farmer Jack's in Troy, MI, we stocked up on dried pinto beans, shredded coconut, long-grain white rice, and canned whole tomatoes.

At Cub Foods in Chicago, IL, we carried out cases of canned corn and green beans along with gallon jugs of blended scotch whiskey and gin.

She once filled an entire suitcase with dry ice and shrimp fresh off the boat in New Orleans, LA, before driving us back home to Jamaica, Queens, NY.

DJ: And where is your grandmother now?

CALLER: Right here beside me waiting for her song.

AN ARCHEOLOGY OF DREAMS

AN ARCHEOLOGY OF DREAMS

AN ARCHEOLOGY OF DREAMS

AN ARCHEOLOGY OF DREAMS

ELIOT WEINBERGER

FALL 1998

[The North, c. 1000]

Þorbjörg of Indriðastaðir dreamed that eighty wolves passed by with flames coming from their mouths, and among them was a white bear.

Glaumvör dreamed that a bloody sword was sticking out from her husband's tunic, and that a river ran through the house, sweeping away all their things.

Hersteinn Blund-Ketilsson dreamed he saw his father on fire.

Ásmundr Kappabani dreamed that a group of women stood over him, holding weapons, and said: "You are expected to be a leader, yet you fear eleven men."

King Gormr dreamed that three black oxen came out of the sea, ate the grass down to the roots, and went back to the sea. Then he heard a great crash.

Bárðr dreamed that a giant tree grew from his father's hearth, covered with blossoms, and that one of the branches was solid gold.

Gísli dreamed he went to a house, filled with friends and relatives, and they sat by seven fires, some flaming brightly and some nearly burnt out. He dreamed that a woman came to him on a gray horse and invited him to her house; they rode together, and went inside, and there were soft cushions on the seats. Then he dreamed that another woman came, and washed his head in blood.

Blindr dreamed he saw King Haddingr's falcon with all its feathers plucked out.

Guðrún dreamed she was wearing an ugly hat; she wanted to take it off, but people told her not to, so she pulled it off her head and threw it in a brook. She dreamed she was standing by a lake, wearing a silver ring on her arm which slipped off into the water. She dreamed she was wearing a gold ring on her arm which slipped off, hit a rock, broke into pieces, and the pieces began to bleed. She dreamed she was wearing a gold helmet, set with precious stones, and that it was so heavy she could not walk.

Kostbera dreamed that the sheets of her husband's bed were on fire.

Þorkell Eyjólfsson dreamed his beard was so large it covered the land.

Þorgils Örrasbeinsstjúper dreamed he looked at his knee, and five leeks were growing out of it.

Þorgils Böðvarsson dreamed that a tall woman came to his door, wearing a child's cloak, and she was very sad.

Hálfdan dreamed he had hair more beautiful than anyone, that it grew in all colors and all lengths: some fell down to his knees, some to his hips, some to his shoulders, and some were merely tufts.

Ragnhildr dreamed she took a thorn out of her smock and it grew from her hand into a great tree that was red at the bottom, green in the middle, and snow-white at the top.

Þorsteinn Surtr dreamed he was awake but everyone else was asleep; then he dreamed he fell asleep and everyone else woke up.

Þorsteinn Uxafótr dreamed that a burial mound opened and a man dressed in red came out. He greeted him pleasantly and invited him into his house. They descended into the mound, which was well furnished. On his right he saw eleven men, sitting on a bench, dressed in red. On his left he saw twelve men, sitting on a bench, dressed in blue.

King Sverrir dreamed that a man came to his bed and told him to follow. They walked out of town and into the countryside, where

they came to a fire on which a man was being roasted. The guide told him to sit and eat, and gave him a roasted human leg. He ate reluctantly, but with each bite he enjoyed it more, and couldn't stop eating.

Jón, bishop of Hólar, dreamed that he was praying before a large crucifix, that Jesus bent down and whispered something in his ear, but he did not understand the words.

Þuríðr Þorkelsdóttir dreamed that her dead husband appeared and told her not to think ill of her son-in-law.

Flosi dreamed that he and his friends were in Lómagnúpr, looking at the mountain. Then the peak opened, and a man came out, wearing a goatskin jacket and carrying an iron staff. He called each of the men by his name. Flosi asked him what the news was, and the man told him there wasn't any.

Án the Black dreamed that a repulsive woman appeared by his bed, cut out his entrails, and stuffed his body with brushwood. Then he dreamed that she took out the brushwood and put his entrails back.

Þórhaddr Halfjótsson dreamed his tongue was so long it wound around his neck.

Sturla Sighvatsson told his friend that he had dreamed that he had a sausage in his hand, that he had straightened it out, broken it in half with his hands, and given half to this same friend. Moreover, he knew that the dream was occurring now, in the same moment of time in which he was telling the dream to his friend, holding a sausage in his hand.

King Atli dreamed that the reeds he wanted to grow were torn up by the roots, reddened in blood, brought to his table, and given him to eat. He dreamed he ate the hearts of hawks, with honey.

A man from Skagafjörðr dreamed he came into a great house where two women were rocking. They were covered with blood, and blood rained on the windows.

Þorleifr Þorgilsson dreamed his sister gave him a piece of cheese, and that all the crust was cut off it.

PARTS OF A BODY

PARTS OF A BODY

PARTS OF A BODY

PARTS OF A BODY

PARTS OF A BODY

SHAWN WEN

FALL 2010

"I hope you are not going to ask me my life story, because, well, everyone knows it already."

Young Marceau

He imitated anything he could think of
It wasn't imitation, it was play
It wasn't play
He was a bird
He took the shapes of plants and trees
He spoke silence, the language of fish
The body was boneless
Loose like elastic
He could have held the form of anything that vibrated and throbbed

Be Caesar
Be Napoleon
Be Robinson Crusoe
Be Charlie Chaplin

He asked, "Must the artist be the fool of society? Does he exist just to make us smile?"

He was a quiet boy. Shy. His schoolwork was immaculate. And he burned to perform.
When he was seven, the children of his neighborhood stood outside his house begging him to turn tricks. When he was nine, he was the main attraction at his aunt's summer camp.

His father was a Jew.
His father's name was Mangel, not Marceau.
His father was a butcher.

His father was a communist.
His father was taken to Auschwitz.
His father's body was taken to the crematorium before his name was recorded in the log.

September 1939
Germany invaded Poland. The day France entered the War, the people of Strasbourg were told they had two hours to pack sixty pounds of belongings each. Marcel was sixteen. He and his brother Alain were among the first to flee.

His brother became a leader of the Underground in Limoges. Marcel, a forger. With red crayons and black ink, he skewered identity papers. He shaved years off the ages of still-tender French children, making them too young to be sent to concentration camps. He dressed them up as boy scouts and campers. He held their hands as they went high into the Alps. Over the mountain and through the woods; out of occupied France and into Switzerland.

1944
His father was captured. He died.
His brother's name appeared on a wanted list on the wall of Gestapo headquarters.
Marcel Mangel left Limoges for Paris and changed his name to Marceau.

In Paris, he joined Jean-Louis Barrault's theater company and Barrault cast him as Harlequin.

Harlequin, the most popular character in the commedia dell'arte:
In Italian, *Arlecchino*
From the Latin *Herculinus*
"Little Hercules"
A hero
The namesake of the Harlequin novel
The lover of Columbina

Standing behind Harlequin, Pierrot pines for Columbina. Barrault himself played this role in *Les Enfants du Paradis*. He is the sad-faced clown dressed in white. The trusting fool. The butt of pranks. The naive, moonstruck dreamer. Ultimately, Columbina breaks his heart and runs away with Harlequin.

1947
Bip was born.

The Bip pantomimes:
Bip in the subway
Bip the street musician
Bip at a society party
Bip commits suicide
Bip as a china salesman
Bip takes an ocean voyage
Bip as a lion tamer
Bip as a painter
Bip as a skater
Bip hunts butterflies
Bip as the botany professor
Bip at the dance hall
Bip plays David and Goliath
Bip as the tailor in love
Bip makes dynamite
Bip the big game hunter
Bip as a matador
Bip goes to an audition
Bip as a soldier
Bip at the restaurant
Bip dreams he is Don Juan
Bip as a babysitter
Bip looks for a job on New Year's Eve
Bip goes to the moon
Bip and the bumble bee
Bip as a fireman
Bip has a sore finger

The theater critic Edward Thorpe wrote for the *Standard*, "I must confess to never having liked Bip anyway. Despite the debt to Chaplin,
the character is close to Pierrot and the winsome whimsical comedia
dell'arte crew, with his affected walks, limp-wristed manner, silly hats
and bizarre costumes that look like a cross between little Lord Fauntle-
roy and an eighteenth century sailor."

1955
He came to New York for a two-week run. He left six months later. He
was originally slated to perform at the Phoenix Theater. From there,

he moved to the Ethel Barrymore on Broadway. From there, the City Center.

The applause begins before he steps onstage
A white figure in the black deep
White
Because it shows movement
White
Because it hides the wrinkles
White
Because we are frail
White
The anguished, drawn-on lines of his face
The face of a clown

He spent his life explaining how his adult body maintained its soft-jointed looseness.
Critics remarked: It's amazing! The man does not age.
But he was never young.

Clive Barnes said, "How we love the invisible mantel shelves he so casually leans against."

The contents of his house:
Icons
Russian boxes
Pre-Columbian sculpture
Mexican pottery
Japanese dolls
Lead soldiers
Toys
Masks

May 1970, Hanoi
"I had the feeling there was no war going on, so kind were the people and so warm the welcome."

Countries Marcel Marceau toured:

Algeria	Hungary	Philippines
Argentina	Iceland	Poland
Australia	India	Portugal
Austria	Indonesia	Romania
Belgium	Iran	Scotland
Brazil	Ireland	Singapore
Canada	Israel	South Africa
Ceylon	Italy	South Korea
Chile	Japan	Spain
China	Lebanon	Sweden
Colombia	Luxembourg	Switzerland
Cuba	Malaysia	Thailand
Cyprus	Morocco	Tunisia
Czechoslovakia	Mexico	United States
Denmark	Netherlands	Uruguay
England	New Zealand	USSR
Finland	Norway	Venezuela
France	Pakistan	Vietnam
Germany	Peru	Yugoslavia

November 1970, New York City
He publicly broke his silence by reading excerpts of *War and Peace* on the radio.

He was married and divorced three times:
Huguette Mallet, two sons, Michel and Baptiste
Ella Jaroszewicz, no children
Anne Sicco, two daughters, Camille and Aurélia

He said, "I was not the greatest father. I was too busy flying around the world."

He bought a farmhouse in Berchéres, an hour outside Paris. There were four trees on the land when he moved there. When he died, there were more than 3,000.

He said, "I am a prisoner of my art. People do not want to see me speak, or use props or appear as a character other than Bip or the styl-

ized mime that I have created. They are uneasy with a Marceau that is unfamiliar."

In 1974, Marcel Marceau did an ad for Xerox's new color copier. The commercial runs for 90 seconds. Marceau mimics a robot. He pantomimes copying both sides of a sheet of paper and pushing the computer around the office. The commercial ends with a promise. He says, "Call Marcel Marceau. If no one answers, it's me."

※

The black stage is a universe without laws. It is up to the mime to conjure and rearrange. It is his to make the dark space become alive with recognitions and quickenings. To him, it is not dark, it is not space. Nothing itself is animated into a wall, a woman, a restaurant, a butterfly, a thief. He can hold out his two empty arms and motion that the world fits in between his hands. All of planet Earth floats in the arm span of one man.

On his relationship to speech

Studs Terkel said, "Only one guy outtalked me. Marcel Marceau. I couldn't get a word in."

Marcel Marceau's first wife divorced him in 1958. She said he would not speak to her for days and days. She called it mental cruelty. He called it rehearsal.

His third wife, Anne Sicco called mime "his only way of thinking and expressing himself."

He used his hands as he spoke.

He said, "I don't suffer from silence. I could be two days without speaking. I wouldn't suffer at all."

There used to be a rumor that he was a deaf mute. He dispelled this rumor by appearing on talk shows: Johnny Carson, Flip Wilson, and Merv Griffin.

He said, "I'm obliged to talk. I don't like to talk especially."

Marcel Marceau had a reputation as a nonstop talker offstage. Those who conversed with him found his conversation as entertaining as his stage performance. His English was nearly flawless, tinged with a French accent.

He said, "I think I am not so different from other people in my private life. Except that I don't like very much to socialize. I am rather a person who is on his own, I like to paint, I like to read, to write, and I travel so much, you know?"

There is a joke that Marcel Marceau released an album. The record consists of twenty minutes of silence followed by applause.

The critic Jeff Bradley wrote: "If Marceau ever decided to make such an album, that's how it would sound, except that the silent spots would be filled with laughs, sighs, an occasional sob."

Marcel Marceau did not like to reveal his original last name. "Mangel" was too common in France. Too many people came forward, claiming to be related to him.

He took the name Marceau from a general in Napolean's army.

He said, "Everyone in the Underground changed his name. You had to in order to survive."

In an interview, Marceau recited lines from his own reviews. He said, "'Marceau explains why theater exists, where it comes from and why it will be with us for a long time.'"

Walter Kerr actually wrote, "Marceau really explains where the theater came from, why it is going to last for a very long time, and why we like it."

Similar. Close enough. But Kerr did not write *Marceau explains why theater exists*. That was all Marceau.

Perhaps his misquote was not unfair. From a man who said that words are deceitful. From a man who said that words are not enough. From a man who said, "If I do the fish, I become the fish, I breathe the water."

✖

Bip is not the bull. Only the matador. Not the bull. To the side of the bullring, Bip the matador keeps a crumpled stovepipe hat with a rose sticking out of it. He may wear the matador's standard three-pointed hat on his head. But the classic Bip hat is there — almost as a reminder. Even when he kills bulls, he is still a poet and a romantic.

He dances, and it's all body. He's like a parading spider. The sweep of his arms conjures up a full stadium on the empty black stage. The bull has stage fright. It doesn't want to come forward. Slapstick, and Bip's pride is undermined. The failed expectations prick against his chest. Chagrin. Chagrin. Bip coaxes the bull. He drags it across the floor. But then, in a twist of his body, Bip sidesteps to serious. In a moment, he is fierce. He spears the bull.

Were you horrified? Did you think he wouldn't actually do it? Bip throws off the matador hat for his own. The stovetop hat. The rose, the rose. He is no longer the killer. Again, the clown.

On the predecessor

Children playing without words, as if dumbstruck in the streets. Children playing without words, starstruck.

Marceau said, "How far back can I summon memories of the past? When I was five years old, my mother took me to see Charlie Chaplin's silent moving pictures. Ah, Chaplin! To us he was a god. He made us laugh and cry, purged us of our own misfortunes, showed us a thousand tricks. And, always, no matter how beaten down, he triumphed over his tribulations in the end."

The first mime company did not rehearse. They were children on parade. Children flying banners fashioned from tattered handkerchiefs. Children wielding tree branches as rifles and canes. Waterloo in front of them. Narrow streets behind them. A dozen little Little Tramps battling the police.

In Paris, Marcel Marceau met Charlie Chaplin. He recognized the aging film star at the Orly Airport. It was 1967. More than fifty years after the first Little Tramp film; more thirty years after the last. Forty years after the advent of talkies dented Chaplin's career for good. Twenty years after the actor was accused of un-American activities. Twenty years after J. Edgar Hoover asked the FBI to keep secret files

on him. Fifteen years after he left the United States for what he thought would be a brief trip. He was not allowed back in.

In 1967, Chaplin was nearing eighty. His fame was diminished, as was his health. No one else recognized him. Marceau's career was strong. The young mime was making television appearances and signing book deals. He approached Chaplin. And after talk of the weather, Marceau began to imitate the Little Tramp. Then Chaplin imitated Marceau's Little Tramp. Marceau brought his knees to the ground, took the Tramp's hand in his own, and kissed it. He looked up to see Chaplin's cheeks wet with tears.

A photographer had accompanied Marceau to the airport. During the meeting with Chaplin, the photographer motioned to Marceau to ask if he should take a picture. Marceau waved him away.

※

Bip struggles against wind that isn't there. He is conjuring this force by stiffening his body. Ducking against the strength of the gust. Digging his heels into the black stage floor. He brought this wind here. He is controlling the weather, itself. Sky and water submit.

No. Not so. Walking against the wind, *pretending* to walk against the wind, he is less effective than you. You, on your way to work, proud as you set your feet to the ground, step by step, day by day.

Is he being? Or is he representing?
Is he   ?

On a tightrope, he is buoyant. The entire stage floor is a string. It's a millimeter wide. It bends and springs.

Is he   ?
Is he playing?

In writing they say, "Show, don't tell."

You do not write, "Bip is impatient."

You write, "Bip taps his feet, and looks all around him. He sways his arms, his fingertips barely grazing the sides of his legs. He rolls his eyes at his date, gesturing toward the door."

Even words are asked to be more than descriptive. They cannot just represent. They cannot sit pretty and let the reader do the work. Even the words try to inhabit. To set a scene.

Then the writer is just a wannabe actor. The actor can twist and bend. Now he is a bird. Now he is a flower. Writers must spell it out. F-L-O-W-E-R. And still, it's just a word. It can't dance. It can't run. It can't fall. You can read it. You can do so much as to pro-nounce it. Try to taste the sibilants as your tap your tongue against your teeth. But you still lack the shape and presence of a body.

On the unwritten book

Marcel Marceau signed a book deal in 1965 to write an autobiography. He titled this book *My Silent Cry*. It was slated for release in 1970. It did not come out in 1970.

In 1983, he said in an interview, "Now they are desperate. But I don't think the book is late. It's ripe to come out now. I feel I'm in my prime. If I had died during the sixties, I would not have been 'achieved.' I know time is running out. I have now 10 years of full power. If I'm not better now than I was 10 years ago I would have stopped. How could I tell? The public."

But the book did not come out in 1983 either. It had not come out by 2007, the year that he died. And the world would never know what Marcel Marceau cried about, openly or privately, in silence or out loud.

On crying

Bip never cries. Bip doesn't exactly "take it like a man." He is too sensitive for that. But he never weeps open tears. When the butterfly's wings stop flapping, when it wilts in his fingers, when it changes its form to more insect and less flower, the corners of Bip's lips turn down. His eyes hollow out. He turns into a mannequin. But he doesn't cry.

Pedrolino is sometimes portrayed as a servant. More often, he is the youngest son, the baby of the family.

Pedrolino cries. He cries when his wife Franceschina is unfaithful, shedding tears of guilt for crimes he did not commit. He cries when he

is caught and punished for playing tricks on Pantaloon and the Doctor, tricks he himself was tricked into playing. He cries when he is beaten by his masters. He cries when he is given a plate of spaghetti, more and more tears streaming down his face with each bite.

He cries and he is not given a mask to hide. His face is powdered white. White to show movement. White to enhance the expressions. White and white alone to give him a range the others are denied.

※

Why this black box? The empty space? Why always perform in a darkened, scraped-out spot?

The mime whirls his arms in the air. His gestures leave a trail: the awning, the veranda, the colonnade. A ghosted landscape rises up wherever his fingers point.

Of course, first there was nothing. Before there was a thing, there was nothing. The earth was formless and empty. Such was the base. God created the world in dark space. The matter that we touch, see, and feel — the architecture and the moss — those were the mistakes.

Silence filters the relationship between words. Between human beings. Every speech is full of empty holes. Text is pockmarked with spaces. No matter how hard we try, the things that exist will never outnumber the things that do not exist.

69 RESTRICTIONS

69 RESTRICTIONS

69 RESTRICTIONS

69 RESTRICTIONS

69 RESTRICTIONS

JOE WENDEROTH

FALL 1997

No person shall be provided with genitalia unless:

1) said person is able to applaud believably
2) said person is appreciative of sunlight in at least most cases
3) said person is continually founded in a series of obvious nondescript colors
4) said person is in possession of an alternative to tonguing
5) said person is willing to apply forever
6) said person has demonstrated a negligible concern for the notion of industrial tenacity
7) said person believes, at bottom, in one thing
8) said person can resist the ugly selfishness of intentional celibacy
9) said person has some experience with creating and/or maintaining the snug
10) said person is pleased by the idea of having a "bottom" and is willing to debate to preserve the idea
11) said person is made hungry by the foul echo, even as he or she understands it as predominately, and ultimately, inedible
12) said person is prone to at least one kind of destructive pouting
13) said person is fit, trim, and undecided
14) said person lacks genitalia
15) said person has "a lot" of personality
16) said person can guarantee that the provision of genitalia will disrupt, and ultimately disallow, the "success" of his or her career
17) said person is made antsy by the sale of safety-insuring devices
18) said person is able to sleep at least one hour (sixty consecutive minutes) per day

19) said person does not in any sense relish resembling his or her parents

20) said person is willing to see genitalia as a kind of modern extension of the alphabet

21) said person can gesture in the general direction of his or her doom

22) said person looks forward to seeing the genitalia of others

23) said person can remain calm in the onset of definitive permission

24) said person is capable of moving, humming, and thrusting as though determined

25) said person feels bound to be clean and to settle down amid clean others

26) said person can differentiate between male and female genitalia and when it is important to do so

27) said person is not intimidated by the gentle sound of unmanned machinery poking the sleeping body of posterity for no reason

28) said person does not object to swelling, except when it interferes with speech or sleep

29) said person is able to remain awake for at least one hour (sixty consecutive minutes) per day

30) said person is able to stop what he or she is doing

31) said person is awed by the consistent discretion evident in the teeming heap of bygones

32) said person wants to live, if by "live" one means *resonate with difficulty*

33) said person is more hopeful when talk is not allowed

34) said person can describe his last meal

35) said person owns a vehicle made entirely of deceased family

36) said person is willing to swear allegiance to whatever is appropriate, even if this means abandoning his or her entire wardrobe

37) said person is capable of understanding climax as the simple disruption of property

38) said person is capable of demonstrating, without a word (as in charades), the very real difference between the womb and the farm

39) said person possesses a reasonably recent Baby Stain Removal Guide

40) said person agrees to forfeit the right to sue with regard to length, depth, or coloration

41) said person is able to sleep at the drop of a hat
42) said person is able to stand his or her own aptitude in the realm of procreation
43) said person knows at least one person (excluding family and sexual partners) by name, and is willing to report that person to the proper authorities (when it is possible to determine the proper authorities)
44) said person feels confident about determining the proper authorities
45) said person is not a freak, if we understand "freak" to mean any person under the sway of an eidos that is insufficiently homogeneous
46) said person speaks in such a way as to conceal the several moistnesses he or she is loosely but momentously tethered to
47) said person has penetrated his- or herself by accident in the past
48) said person is vaguely fond of variety in what is perishable
49) said person is willing to submit his or her conception of animal hierarchy to constant violent doubt
50) said person is willing to insert a finger into an other
51) said person does not mind repetitive work
52) said person has always forded the various soft racks without being reduced to their seeming confluence
53) said person is not without critical holes
54) said person is of a mind to compose music for pornography
55) said person can enthusiastically deny having ever been anywhere
56) said person has penetrated his- or herself on purpose in the past
57) said person loves to appear *available* in the deepest sense
58) said person feels bound to sing and bound to dwindle at the same time, which is to say, feels the future as just that part of the present that, in allowing itself to be carefully misunderstood, prolongs the fictitious flavor its real parasites will not survive on
59) said person stands in a certain way
60) said person is offended by the idea of reasonable foundations
61) said person has demonstrated an unusual grip on the usual, and is fond of reminiscing upon this demonstration

62) said person has a can-do attitude when it comes to creating the circumstances in which it is possible to drown
63) said person is conspicuously without blame with regard to the specific course taken by that which resists extinction almost successfully
64) said person feels his or her head looks "just right"
65) said person believes the word "person" signifies, above all, a mobile, vacant, and consistently endangered habitat
66) said person is melting
67) said person needs a place to stay
68) said person is a qualified but uncertifiable damage-sound coordinator
69) said person is willing to swear that he or she will adhere to all written restrictions, and to the spirit of hampered freedom in general

Note: Other restrictions may apply. All restrictions are subject to endless disintegration and/or increasing clarification.

THE DRY DANUBE:
A HITLER FORGERY

THE DRY DANUBE:
A HITLER FORGERY

THE DRY DANUBE:
A HITLER FORGERY

THE DRY DANUBE:
A HITLER FORGERY

PAUL WEST

SPRING 2000

Here I come, slinking brickward in the hour of lavender, to what I call my sentry box, a niche in a wall really, opposite a restaurant called Terza Rima. Brick above me, to one side decrepit stone, behind me ironwork of indeterminate design as of a garden gate mangled. It is where I observe the evening comings and goings of those who can afford Terza Rima (here too a three-shrimp appetizer for the price of several oxen). I leave my hovel, wondering why, in a place so scruffy, there is the continual smell of new paint, which must well up from some channel in the building, and quite apart from what I am told is my own characteristic body odor: engine smoke, as in railroad, somewhat sulfurous and sooty. Here I lurk, a born lurkster, hoping perhaps to spot Treischnitt and Kolberhoff arriving to spend their ill-gotten pelf, little pondering the fate of those living on the fringe, unable to eat friendship, doomed to fill the belly with water from the local pump, to wash and shave in the same place. They have, as it were, gone beyond, confining themselves to a studio of veil-lit northern aspect, in which the light seems no longer a priceless gift from an uncaring Creator. Myself, I paint in the semi-darkness, which is no doubt what they picked up in my Auersberg and disliked so much, the lack of light falling on the people's heads, that commonplace benison. Carriages arrive, honking autos, with money striding out of them on the prowl for three-shrimp appetizer, bitter aperitif, creamy desserts from which oozes the white worm of luxury. The lurkster inhales their perfume, their cologne, their leather and silk, wishing he had not attended that grisly interview with Treischnitt and Kolberhoff, who after all were not the personages billed as in charge. Somehow, they shuffled themselves into position merely to "get" me, relinquishing their chairs as soon as I vanished. Surely their offered carrot of a Fisher King Fellowship was bogus, a final taunt, retaliation for my hounding them; but you never know, the whole thing might have been accidental, and, as ever, I am trying to

make sense of something that makes none but is merely what happened next. What Happened Next, of which the world is full, poorly as we accommodate ourselves to it. Should the pair of them arrive, Treischnitt and Kolberhoff, I would love to over-hear them actually praising my Auersberg, venting the real truth, relieved to admit at last, to each other, the superiority of my work, the legacy from so and so that I have at last fulfilled. Yes, you know, the poor wretch really has something. Awkward, lumbering, maladroit, true, but he really has the real thing. Every mother has one, but this one's a nascent genius. No shunting him off to architecture, no fear; he belongs in the atelier of time, apple of the Academy's eye. Well gentlemen, I am still waiting, and when I barge out of hiding, blistering the night air with my distress, it is as a commissionaire in a topcoat far too big for him, with red and gold epaulets, a fancy hat smothered in festive braid, feet encased in stenchy boots, nose a-run, eyes teeming, hands raw from fending off baggage, my back sore from bowing, my undergarments drenched from standing in the rain all day in the hope of a small coin or two from those over whom I hold an umbrella big as Portugal and just as dry. Beyond such an ap-pointment, at which I huff and puff, ever on the trot, there is only that chore in the basement, to which I am bound eventually to be assigned: toilet man, accustomed to the flush and flatus of an entire civilization. It has not come yet, but soon it will. Com-missionaires are ten a penny, are they not? I can almost imagine Treischnitt and Kolberhoff doing my job for me, a double act, but for now, *qua* painter, I retreat into the shadows again, into my so-called sentry box, determined not to torture myself with dreams of what's to come. There is doom, and there are the little dooms in between: the pre-dooms, about which it is better not to think. Yet how many of us, having no political party to succor us, torment ourselves with the pre-dooms, afraid to envision the fi-nal one, as it were rehearsing the ultimate charade, our insignia an empty plate crossed with a rat skull. The thousands of us who gather in the dusk, out of sight, our hopes as loud as the twitter-ings of bats, we stand and pray for something nobler to end with, having been besmirched by the Treischnitts and Kolberhoffs in this or that miserable calling, yet through sheer persistence at-tuned to the side chatter of disembarking fat cats who depart heavier by several kilos of gravy, cream, steak, kidney, shrimp, and lard. A mere sampling would suit us, get us through the: night, even to inhale: their burps, cognac breath on gravy breath, what a feast, my masters, too rich a diet: fur the lungs of the likes

of us. We'd burp it back, would we not? It's what happens when the empty stomach beholds the full one, and the extra fat wobbling on their ladies' behinds. Just think of all the wet silk trapped in between. I linger on, recognizing not a soul: no artists certainly. I would be better loitering at some café misnamed Des Artistes, at which nonartists search in vain for real artists, who can never afford such dumps. By and large we do not make money. We wince and shrivel, carp and blame, but we do muck our hands with oil and turps, filling in the lonely gaps beneath the nails, wondering how much more we can abide. Few come to get us, though we all believe in rescue by millionaire. Was there not once, is there not to come, a regiment named the Artist's Rifles, perhaps just formed from among the malcontents of London's studios? Against whom? Is it just a bunch of painters eager to kill somebody? I would join if I only knew how. If not them, then the Painters' Brigade, a lordly tide to be sure, a brigade of smotherers who wangle their way at night like cat burglars into the homes of the idle rich and there suffocate them with all the oily rags of yesteryear, much as we would if we worked on locomotives all the day. Simply, the oils smell differently. It is a different division of a world order. Visibly, I live in my imagination, hammering away at what is not quite real, but having little else beyond Trcischnitt and Kolberhoff to keep me going, and my private vision of the Auersberg. You have to have something to hold to, even if only the cap of the milk bottle, within it a flap you push down so as to reach the contents. We are like that, delivered to the doorstep, the stoop, with a little round cap in the center of which there's a smaller cap to shove down, giving access to our inflamed insides. Prod through the cream at the top and get your finger into the milk of human cream. That does it. I am through with metaphor, banned in the Artist's Rifles and replaced by bullets named for dead painters. Shoot someone with a da Vinci, someone else with a Hals. Never mind who, just note the name and shoot. This is how all great revolutions begin, with a bitter man in a doorway, empty and cold, his features graced by a current of lavender light from high above, his eyes gloom-adapted, his life's work rolled up into a cylinder in a nameless attic to which not even mice have climbed. I exaggerate. It would be poetic justice if Treischnitt and Kolberhoff were to arrive now, disgorging themselves from an ornate carriage, both got up in commissionaire uniforms, the tailor by royal appointment to the Academy. These men do not so much control Art, they *are* Art. It makes you sick to think of it. Time to move to a different door-

way before the police lay hands on me, huffily saying Time now, good fellow, to darken some other spot. You'll need help from an unexpected quarter now, which they say as "Yewl need elp from ha diffrunt kwor-a." What kind of lingo is that? I have been moved on much more than I have ever moved myself, easily (to put it in vivid terms) all the way from Vienna to Istanbul, rather than from Istanbul to Ankara. And on foot too. Imagine that. The shoe leather becomes the merest abstraction, so thin and translucent you can read newspaper through the soles provided you tread on it first. We do not so much walk on rugs as grace them with our sole-prints, becoming experts in texture (Persian, Turkish, et cetera), able to tell blindfolded which rugs are worn, and by whom, and which are not. Sidewalks scar us and roads make us bleed, we the sensitive contingent placed on the planet to bother it while it shields itself from the accumulated sadness of collapsing civilization ripe for a dunt. Shall we be part of that? Bet your pfennig we will, there being little else to do other than endorsing checks and visiting bank managers about the rate of compound interest. Treischnitt and Kolberhoff suddenly arrive, as if summoned up by some incantation, not this, and disappear into Terza Rima like two airships in dalmatics. One of them is gaunt and narrow, Treischnitt, but he seems to have fattened up for this outing. Forever talking about me, and eager to sit down troughing while doing so, they leave behind them like shreds of bird feather the usual tributes, and I almost bow, imagining the praise they muster, too shy in their heart of hearts to say it to my face. So do we all die, trying to better ourselves, trying to cheer ourselves up, not as if Treischnitt and Kolberhoff, two rampant mediocrities, ruled the world, but as if Treischnitt and Kolber- hoff *were* the world, that foul maze of people who never do their jobs or respond or really work, but miscellaneously get by be- cause they trust one another, all being much the same, even when they drop dead. The stink is much the same, the plug in the backside, to stave off the avalanche that so worried the great Goethe, the same for all. We are only bags of it in different plac- es with varying labels. If I said all this out loud, I'd be in real trouble, beating at the bars to get out in time for my ninetieth birthday, one last look at Treischnitt and Kolberhoff, choking on buttercream torte, ever regnant, the semi-kings, the lickers of all private ice creams. Away I shuffle, envying anyone his bicycle, yet determined to wait it out. I no sooner moved than I wished I had stayed put. In their full glory appeared the little outdoor tables, sheathed in white cloths, over which sippers rather than

diners huddled as if over altars, their voices for the most part hushed, their gestures curbed. There was something mysterious about this hour, spring or fall, I can rarely tell which, and I wished I were part of the perpetual ongoing confab that ruled the world, knew of all the crannies and intervals, the hidey-holes and the secret bank accounts. I would have behaved myself, back ramrod stiff, forelock combed back and moored with lemon curd, eyes bathed to leech out the red. So I stepped back, thinking this could go on for a lifetime without anyone's noticing me or telling me, in the mode of the place, to get a move on. Perhaps if they saw me at all they took me for a statue, even a virgin in her shawl or a saint about to be boiled in oil. I was there, but in a sense I was not, I was only Treischnitt's and Kolberhoff's solitary retainer, watching their spears and arrows for them until they resumed the hunt for greatness. What if I sat down without bidding a waiter to seat me, omitting the customary tip that went with the favor, even before you have begun ordering. The logic of life in that place was something like this: I am breathing, so here's a tip for you, thank you very much. Keep me alive. I suddenly wanted to get back to my wooden fork, the holed tablecloth (ravaged linoleum), the wobbly chair, the little stenchy larder that held a breadbin and a cheese cage — as if the cut would get up and walk away propelled, or is it impelled, by its own maggots. I needed no music, no apéritif, no company, beyond Treischnitt and Kolberhoff, nothing on the walls save anyone of my aborted works of art. Nor much light, even though I saved the candle's drippings and rolled a tiny offspring cored by a single hair. It never worked, the delirious idea of the potent miniature held sway in my brain as something to patent and one day make me a fortune. Hours I had spent in there, drawing almost in the dark, feeling my way through cornices and pediments, sometimes using charcoal I would accidentally rub away with my torn sleeve, which meant I never saw what I had drawn, just a flurry of lines and smoke as if a locomotive had passed nearby. If this was Hovel Number One, would Two be worse? If so, what must I rehearse for? Swat all flies and stamp all beetles until I have a dark brown paste to do my umbers with, smearing the mixture in place with my thumb to give an effect of spurious stucco. That would be the day, when I invented a new technique, such as scumbling, and my name would appear in the ABZ of Art, next to the man who invented pointillisme or tachisme. Such dreams. I have not mentioned the goddesses, dangerous and sublime, who arrive at almost any hour, at a safe distance

looking almost marble or wooden, but intently fixed upon the enormous slash in their anatomy, the badge of their duty and perspective in life. They always have this in mind, whatever else they seem to attend to. I keep them ethereal or I would never get anything done, for their demands are gross once begun, and art, as I know it, has no time for the imperium of the gash, is an altogether different zone of demand and privilege, demanding of you no less than the goddesses the energy of your entire life. Treischnitt and Kolberhoff, the Treischnitts and the Kolberhoffs know this of course, whatever pretensions they have to pipe-smoking at the domestic hearth, ignoring the primal call to go beyond the brown-pink lips at the rim of that cavity factory. Such delving must be for others who ignore the call of Apollo, and they must risk the imputation to them of inhuman motives. One semi-swoons of course in the perfumed aura left behind them by these temptresses, whose single-mindedness matches my own. No man can say he has not come close to losing his divine spark in those eyes, in the folds of flesh they amble about to flaunt, but the most dedicated of us have to keep our mind intact and push our energy into the drab arena of the canvas, the thick paper of ravishing texture. This is where any Stefanie ends up, of course, adored but physically shunted away, although conserved in the mind as an angelic figure on a festive landing in the act of welcoming an evening's friends, the exquisite hostess, to whom countless love poems have been addressed, lauding her as a damsel of high rank, clad in a dark-blue overflowing robe of purest velvet, and, when not on the landing, astride a white palfrey of sheerest delicacy, riding over flower-strewn meadows never trampled before, her loose tresses cascading over her shoulders like a golden flood, above her the bright, keen sky of spring capping a scene of radiant happiness. At such a distance, she: is never torrid, although thinking of her evokes Wagnerian moments that are. One honors and disobeys, couching one's amazement in the gentlest figures, knowing this is the bait in the trap, and our entire populated planet the clue to our failure m resist. Besides, if you have to keep abreast of the Treischnitts and Kolberhoffs, ever on the *qui vive* those two industrious gentlemen, you are too weak for anything else. It is not keeping up with the Joneses, ever reminded of Miss Jones and Mrs. Jones, as my adored British say, but dragging after Treischnitt and Kolberhoff in their incessant forays and endeavors, never if you can help it getting left behind. Have your Rubens cake, but do not eat it except during some elated picnic of the mind, preferably to the tunes of

Rienzi. In the mind's eye some visual echo of Makart while, with some male friend, a Kubizek, you clamber up the Freinberg, there to contemplate the august town lying beneath, and surrender to the tide of images that mounts inside, purges you, and will not leave you be until it has washed you clean with a vision of the future in which you will not lead, of course, though your works will flank the triumphal archway through which the nation marches to glory. Inspired by art, an entire people would forget its pain and mishaps: not exactly the world envisioned by Treischnitt and Kolberhoff, whose feet of clay hold them back, but akin, simply because they have had more time in which to amass sublime images for which as they calculate they will never be forgotten. It is hard, in recounting this, not to think it is happening all over again, thriving in the present and future tenses, instead of being treasured in retrospect as what actually happened before all else, but I dangle between enthusiastic recall and transport back into the moment, all subsequent life erased, only those austere magical moments remaining. Who can be strong enough not to slip back into his youthful ecstasies, glorying in a picture that has no frame but sucks him in for the most delicious amnesia of all? It was like that before I ever went near Vienna, when I was dazzled and captivated as by a collection of fine diamonds, by the Ringstrasse, splendid as Aladdin's Cave, museum upon museum, in which it was possible to imagine my own work installed in the permanent collection. In that trance of overpowering opera and sublime visual visitation, I knew I had the spiritual wherewithal, even if not the financial, but a crescendo awaited me, could I but tear myself away from places almost as beloved, just as my own father had done many years before, resolved to make something of himself as he strode out with scarcely a backward glance. The power to sever, or, if not quite that, to freeze and annul the parts of one's being that hold one back, that is the discipline of the upward climber whom I also call far-ward, the yearner emancipated from his own froth and gearing himself for the kind of applause most men only dream of. For them the arid formulas of schooling, the chapter and verse of a so-called education. My love was the flux, ricochet from God's own indecisiveness, that called out to us to make what we could of this turmoil: to the strongest the prize! Batten on to those who have won and suck their secret from them as during one of those sustained childhood kisses, usually an arm, when you kiss and then suck and suck until the whole area reddens and flecks of blood appear. The blood-kiss we urchins

dubbed it, it left a speckle behind it, perhaps a bruise, but the recipient knew she had been honored and savored. So, I would blood-kiss Treischnitt and Kolberhoff, swiftly gathering up the vital names from gossip and discarded newspapers, aiming myself like a hawk until the chivalrous day I was taken in, "made of their company," and encouraged to continue without having to go through any more of the twizzles that guaranteed the future of the imagination and the heart, all childhood romance left behind me as I towered without teetering, with nary a swagger, even strolling two paces behind Treischnitt and Kolberhoff, inhaling the blood aroma from their exhaled smoke as the wind seized it and elaborated it this and that, knowing I had arrived. Once you have arrived, you endure, you do not always need to work at it, any more than a train, having chugged into Vienna, has to labor further, not even to disgorge. To accomplish this goal, I made my sacrifices, as who does not, but not such as leave a scar, leaving Mama, Mama alive, Mama dead, but the young artist or the young grenadier has to harden himself at some point, even if it takes him a year and a half to condition himself to the stress of leaving. *They* will not go away from *you*, you go away from them. This doctrine, implanted by who knew whom, ultimately enabled me to break away Vienna-ward, where the enviable baubles lay with blank nameplates on their sides. So I Treischnitted and Kolberhoffed, as I said, to my heart's delight, inhaling energy from the very city, until I became the new Treischnitt/Kolberhoff, talk of the town, veering the face of glory as calmly as I did sunlight, aping no one, obliging my hosts by being there: what I longed to think of myself, the young man who, striking out on his own, with only his genius to declare, had actually made it, atop the Reinberg once again. The next thing I did was to pretend to be a civilized-looking sipper at a table, oddly crouching there with a westward view to catch sight of the green flash as it is called, when the sun dips below the horizon and the eye's favorite color crackles triumphantly through as all the other colors give up the ghost. I was a poor imitation, very soon ushered on and away, but I had seen the flash and took it home with me, wondering if I should implant it in some work of mine just to test the mind of the viewer. What had Treischnitt or Kolberhoff said about my Auersberg? Consider the foreground in its own right and ask yourself if the figures bear nobly enough their representative role? Some old bunch of rhubarb like that. I did, I isolated them, at the back of my mind the old medical school canard that said if you are not gifted enough to be a doc-

tor, then become a dentist. In my version, *sotto voce*, it became. If you are not a good enough artist, then become an architect. A fine scandal, that. Well, my figures did look scraggy, apart from the one woman on the left, the others perhaps appealing for help, even the two engaged in pulling-pushing the gurney on which I saw at least two barrels not prevented from rolling about. The whole crew had a windblown look, temporary and torn, perhaps merely a hint of our precarious fate in this world, perhaps an index to my lack of interest, then anyway, in the texture of people's being, as the jargon of the schools puts it. You have to know what you are getting into as the actress said to the bishop. Perhaps I should then, so Treischnitt and Kolberhoff, remove the foreground from the painting and treat it as a theme in its own right, instead of leaving it scraggly and scraggy, reconceiving it as an esplanade crammed with diners and sippers all intent on seeing the green flash, craning and stretching toward the west, but for what who knew? All minimal action (Treischnitt, Kolberhoff) designed to get the viewer wondering and thus involved at the level of fervent interest, rather more than that of an accumulator battery joined to a front-door lamp. Who can that be at the door? The lamp does not care. I could see the bowler hats and gaping corsages of it all, the tiny wind among the mustaches and spit-curls, but for the life of me I could not see the commercialization of that plaza as worth doing. I wanted it empty, almost neglected, to indicate the pomp of the place behind it. But Treischnitt and Kolberhoff had said in different ways, with different hurrumphs, the palace and the plaza before it were both dead, vacant, as appealing to a potential buyer as the stone floor of an abattoir or the suet of an eviscerated beast hung up by its rear knees to drain. Was I going to modify it or not? Scribbling did not help. It would have to be a new work entirely, not a revamped one, I thought, neither Treischnitted nor Kolberhoffed, my masters, whatever pain it put the potential buyer to. My own was just that. What it all came to eventually, as might have been expected, was Treischnitt and Kolberhoff cramping around in the plaza in front of the Auersberg, complaining about the surface to be walked on, not smooth enough, the way the wind roared in and spun around, the way the area included so many vantage points that gave a poor view of the building's symmetry, as if the damned place had designed itself. But this was only their way of being self-important, with ever a misgiving about something of no interest to them. All they wanted to do was be self-important vis-à-vis the likes of me, the aspirant, the nebbish, the

greenhorn, lecturing them about, oh, what were the words they used? Contrast, parallel, even demeanor and style. Imagine anyone correcting the demeanor of a building! Nor was I architect enough to care, but they were certainly animating the empty area in front, and that I supposed was their main point, as if four-handedly they had introduced the Renaissance into the regions of the philistine Huns. All balls, that, but it's what those in power do to you when you are in the silly posture of *applying*, as if you don't know anything, can't learn anything, own no books and have not even a set-square to your name. On they tromp like elephants inspecting a burial ground (yours), and lay down the law with fierce tedium, as sure of themselves as those wardens of San Quentin, that American hell-hole, who had all inmates photographed with a mirror so as to save money by doing front and profile all in one. Some Austrians know their stuff. Thank God I have Treischnitt and Kolberhoff as whipping boys, popping in to steel me when I least expect it. I would prefer Treischnitt if he were more like Kolberhoff, and Kolberhoff if he were more like Treischnitt, who says with a note of hysterical frenzy, Well at least you didn't cram the foreground with rabble, my lad, you show a certain political sense. This was more Kolberhoff than Treischnitt, but Treischnitt got in first, he the intellectual snob, Kolberhoff the social one. I have nothing to say to them. They irk me even at their most ingratiating. Treischnitt at the gallop is almost worse than Treischnitt backed up by Klaus, Odel, and Pfintner, none of whom support Kolberhoff, who counts on five toadies, as he once said to me, not to Treischnitt his crony: Fnenck, von Traub, von Eschpitz, Dünckner, and Klemp. How they keep them straight I do not know. Does either of them sometimes need the other's henchmen? Are there no henchwomen? Is there no one there to speak up for the dregs, the rotters, the people who have no hope, what used to be called the proletariat of the society? The ones who provided the milk and did the suckling — was that it? Let them, so say Treischnitt and Kolberhoff, drink piss, let them trough on shit like dogs, we have to keep society in strict order, such as clearing the foreground of yours truly's palace drawing. Despicable vacancy. Get some thinkers. So Herr Treischnitt. Bring on some carriages, my boy. So Herr Kolberhoff. Who wound these men up? Might they be fused together by lightning? Great God in heaven, says Kolberhoff, in his cups, We know what this working-class hyena will draw whenever he gets the chance, he will empty the scene of the aristocracy, it's as plain as day, only to be corrected by Treischnitt, as often when

addressing Kolberhoff his junior, It is not the aristos he wants out of here, it's the smarty-pants, they upset him because they think all the time and he is accustomed to living among polar bears. Ice-bears, Kolberhoff says, I call them ice-bears, as distinct from bugbears and Russian bears, put him in a pit and prod him with pointed staves. Stop indulging him, Treischnitt, but Treischnitt is having none of that, he is top dog after all, he says. A pox on him, we shouldn't be dealing with the likes of him, it's only a matter of a stipend neither of us needs. I don't need it. Neither do you. No, I don't, Kolberhoff admits. We ought to be off in the Alps picking flowers and greasing our wives' buttocks with pigfat for the grand onslaught up there in the thin air. Well, says Treischnitt, I'll be buggered. No, you won't, says Kolberhoff, but *they* will, if I have anything to do with it, while this tripehound of an aspirant is drawing the palaces of his betters and who knows what filthy comers of the society he comes from and should return to. There are spaces for gentlemen, but none for ragamuffins. Just so, Kolberhoff, says Treischnitt, who often tells Kolberhoff to stuff his mouth but not on this day of days after the judging, was it not, when they are both quite knackered. Now they are talking, I imagine, about how, I imagine, I draw. Imagine that. He seizes the pencil, says Kolberhoff, talking first as he often likes to, Treischnitt's wit being a bit sharper, and chews on it with his brown teeth, wondering what the fuck to depict, which he then does with all kinds of correct angles as if proving Pythagoras. He is all of that, so Treischnitt goes on: Not knowing in whose head all these bloody angles are. He peruses the ground: Kolberhoff. His ground: Treischnitt. Well, fuck his ground: Kolberhoff. He copies: Treischnitt. He copies other drawers: Kolberhoff. Lord I want to throw up, Treischnitt says, he wants to be an artist, he Wants To Be An Artist. Now, what is the Greek for that disease? Balls to Greeks, Kolberhoff says, derivative megalomania I call it. He shuts up. I hear them and want to kill them, these pansy toadies with their balls in their top pockets. Where have they come from? What lousy country estate threw them out? Fat stuffed Austrian pigeons I'd like to roast on a spit, polite to my face, ravaging monsters behind my back. Call me *he*, they do, I have a nobody for a face. My day will come, but it will have a black border printed around it by the coroner, and all the time the heirs of Treischnitt and Kolberhoff are building a newer trousers press to torture me with: pants by Herr Procrustes. Give up the profession of graphite or take the water torture upside down. Who can be a genius in such circumstances?

Only a deadhead would prevail, eyes closed. One of my early mistakes, I realized, had been to gamble all on one drawing, masterstroke or not, when perhaps Treischnitt and Kolberhoff wanted the gamut, all of my moods and ploys in one portfolio: the full man, with not a quirk omitted. So I began to work on another scene from old Vienna, not heirloom palace this time, but a nostalgia-thick corner, say, knowing this would jerk the tear strings. In addition, I tried to keep better track of their movements, Treischnitt and Kolberhoff, which included the dentist and the colonic irrigation clinic, the artist's provision store (they kept buying although they no longer seemed to paint). Their new habit, unless I had previously been unobservant to a severe degree, was to go about apart, or perhaps fifty meters away from one another, in the park or at the coffeehouse, which was bewildering: anyone habituated to Treischnitt-Kolberhoff watching would at once conclude the other was in the offing when he saw only Treischnitt or Kolberhoff, which meant that he would assume the other was close when in fact he might have been far away. Worse, in seeking the other, you might lose the one you already had, so there was an ever-widening gulf for the eye to accommodate, a vast area to scour even if only for Treischnittiana- or Kolberhoffiana-discarded wrappers, bits of tobacco fallen at the smolder and unreclaimed, left to burn on neglected and unsavored. It was a hard, unrewarding time during which I might have popped the question about this or that: how many drawings/paintings to submit next time, whether to tear everything in half and show only the backgrounds or the foregrounds, whether or not if finances ran to such devious extravagance I should sprinkle the right tobacco over the surface, not a lot but an identifiable sprinkling that clung to a thin smear of flour-and-water glue made in the chipped enamel bowl I reserved for all my ablutions. So much entered into the next phase that I wished many a time for a conference with either of them or both, just to air my professional worries and, as it were, steal a march on the market. No such luck. No doubt Treischnitt and Kolberhoff were going about in disguise, in monocles (what did you call two monocles worn at the same time?), huge fur coats, clown rouge and Pagliaccio paste. It was no use asking. Nobody in my acquaintance would believe that in a serious profession such people existed, never doing their jobs, denying they ever had such jobs, certainly claiming they had no dealings with such as me (how many of me were there in Vienna, scuttling like lizards in between the feet of the great as they thundered about in spats?).

Visiting their office was a waste of time: no nameplates, no plates below protected glass, no directions painted on the walls, and no unique after-bouquet in the toilets, that ultimate spoor. I knew the aroma of their afterbirths, so to speak, but no amount of covert sniffing gave me any clue. The two most important men in Vienna had done a bunk, which to anyone in the know meant only that they were doing their work in the usual manner of high-placed, high-ranking eccentrics, to whom work was the merest bagatelle, subject daily to impromptu metamorphosis I called camouflage. They were bound to be somewhere, of course, but I soon ceased looking for two men together and began scrutinizing groups of three or four, even five or six (ideal hiding, this), but with no luck. Ideally, of course, they should have moved, both Treischnitt and Kolberhoff, into my own building to hide right in front of me; unable to believe my own eyes, I would have discounted the evidence of *all* my senses. But that feeble assemblage of bricks and mortar, mainly chips and fungus, hardly qualified as a building anyway, so it was no use expecting miracles. I went on looking, considered stealing someone's dog and training it to find them, but no dog appealed. Can you believe that in the whole of Vienna I could not find a dog worth stealing, with then to follow the entire course of Treischnitt-Kolberhoff training. Why, I wondered, were people appointed to jobs they would never do? Answer came that they got those jobs because they did not need them. Such was the animating principle of most communities. Hence the presence of an enormous rump or leftover, these being the qualified that nobody needed: people with degrees, lifelong experience, a real gift for the job and commitment to it. Feckless amateurs ruled the roost, so was this why many of us decided Vienna was ready for a fall? Other cities behaved in just the same way, the key to the whole maneuver being that the city didn't want to be caught out doing anything obvious. You could tell how advanced a city was from the hordes of frustrated people marching about in search of such and such a person supposedly doing a job — sanitary inspector, maître d', plumber, bricklayer, literary critic, house painter — all in vain. All you ever found was the literary critic, say, with a trowel in his fist, a load of mortar on his shoulder, or the sanitary inspector making marginal notes on a Wagner score. This was surely one form of originality, but it daunted the least adventurous and actually drove some to suicide, all their golden hopes dashed, their promises betrayed. I persisted, having nothing else to hope for, but my Treischnitt and Kolberhoff

forays never paid off like the old ones, and I had to make up my mind without the least guidance or advice. After a while, I began to hear non-conversations from them, Treischnitt telling Kolberhoff to say something to me, and then telling him to tell me he had said nothing at all, closely followed by Kolberhoff telling Treischnitt to tell me something he'd said and soon after telling him to tell me he'd said nothing at all. Then I heard them in unison, telling each other to tell me something they had said or wanted to say, and then canceling it by telling each other to tell me that they had not said it at all. This was the Great Oral Wall of China. Past this there was no going, and there will be never.

ABOUT THE CONTRIBUTORS

ABOUT THE CONTRIBUTORS

ABOUT THE CONTRIBUTORS

ABOUT THE CONTRIBUTORS

ABOUT THE CONTRIBUTORS

ABOUT THE CONTRIBUTORS

Eula Biss is the author of *The Balloonists, Notes from No Man's Land*, and *On Immunity: An Innoculation*. The recipient of numerous awards, including a National Endowment for the Arts fellowship, a Guggenheim Fellowship, and the National Book Critics Circle Award, her work has appeared in anthologies such as *The Best American Nonrequired Reading, The Best Creative Nonfiction*, and the *Touchstone Anthology of Contemporary Nonfiction*. She teaches creative writing at Northwestern University.

Jenny Boully is the author of *The Book of Beginnings and Endings, The Body: An Essay, [one love affair]*, Not Merely Because of the Unknown That Was Stalking Toward Them*, and *of the mismatched teacups, of the single-serving spoon*. Widely anthologized, Boully's work can be found in *The Best American Poetry, The Best American Essays, The Great American Prose Poem*, and *The Next American Essay*. She teaches creative writing at Columbia College in Chicago.

Anne Carson has published numerous award-winning books, including *Short Talks, Glass, Irony and God, Plainwater: Essays and Poetry, Autobiography of Red, The Beauty of the Husband: A Fictional Essay in 29 Tangos, NOX*, and several translations. The recipient of fellowships from the Guggenheim Foundation, the Lannan Foundation, and the American Academy in Berlin, Carson teaches Classics and Comparative Languages at the University of Michigan.

John D'Agata is the author of *Halls of Fame, About a Mountain, The Lifespan of a Fact*, and a series of anthologies on the history of the essay, the final installment of which is forthcoming from Graywolf Press. He directs the Nonfiction Writing Program at the University of Iowa.

Katie Ford is the author of *Deposition, Storm, Colosseum*, and *Blood Lyrics*. The recipient of fellowships from the Pen American

Center, the American Academy of Poets, and the Lannan Foundation, Ford's work has been published in the *American Poetry Review*, *Ploughshares*, *Partisan Review*, *Seneca Review*, *Poets & Writers*, *American Literary Review*, and *Pleiades*. Poetry editor of the *New Orleans Review*, she teaches creative writing at the University of California at Irvine.

Michael Ives is the author of *The External Combustion Engine*. His work with the performance trio F'loom has been featured on National Public Radio, the CBC, and in the anthology of international sound poetry, *Homo Sonorus*. His poetry and prose has appeared in such magazines as *Conjunctions*, *Denver Quarterly*, *Exquisite Corpse*, *New American Writing*, *Seneca Review*, and *Sulfur*. The recipient of the Lillian Fairchild Award for significant contribution to the arts, Ives teaches creative writing at Bard College.

Wayne Koestenbaum is the author of sixteen books of poetry, fiction, and nonfiction, among them *The Queen's Throat: Opera, Homosexuality, and the Mystery of Desire*, *Jackie Under My Skin*, *Humiliation*, *My 1980s and Other Essays*, *Ode to Anna Moffo and Other Poems*, *Best-Selling Jewish Porn Films*, and *Moira Orfei in Aigues-Mortes*. The recipient of numerous awards, including the "Discovery"/The Nation Poetry Prize and a Whiting Writer's Award, Kostenbaum is Distinguished Professor of English at the City University of New York.

Richard Kostelanetz has published a number of highly experimental books, including *In the Beginning*, *Short Fictions*, *More Short Fictions*, *Furtherest Fictions*, *Autobiographies*, *Visual Language*, *I Articulations*, *Wordworks*, and *More Wordworks*. The recipient of fellowships from the National Endowment for the Arts, the Guggenheim Foundation, the Vogelstein Foundation, and the Pollock-Krasner Foundation, Kostelanetz works out of his studio in Bushwick, New York.

Ander Monson is the author of *Other Electricities*, *Vacationland*, *Neck Deep and Other Predicaments*, *Vanishing Point: Not a Memoir*, and *The Available World*. The recipient of the John C. Zacharis First Book Award and the Christopher Isherwood Foundation fellowship, Monson is the editor of the online journal *DIAGRAM* and teaches creative writing at the University of Arizona.

Mary Ruefle is the author of *The Most of It, Trances of the Blast, A Little White Shadow, Tristimania, Among the Musk Ox People, Apparition Hill, Cold Pluto, Post Meridian, The Adamant, Life Without Speaking, Memling's Veil, Madness, Rack, and Honey,* and *Selected Poems.* The recipient of an Award in Literature from the American Academy of Arts and Letters, a Guggenheim Fellowship, a National Endowment for the Arts fellowship, and a Whiting Writers Award, Ruefle teaches creative writing at Vermont College.

Genevieve Turkett teaches Senior English in Birmingham, Alabama, at Shades Valley High School. She has taken her love of writing out of the publishing world and into the classroom to give support and encouragement to the next generation of great writers. Look for her new book one day about turning a group of misfit high school kids into writing contest winners, or something like that.

Wendy Walters is the author of *Troy Michigan, Longer I Wait, More You Love Me, Birds of Los Angeles,* and a forthcoming collection of essays from Sarabande Books. The recipient of fellowships from the New York Foundation for the Arts, the Ford Foundation, and the Smithsonian Institution, Walters's work has appeared in numerous journals, including *The Iowa Review, Bookforum, Seneca Review, FENCE,* and *Harper's.* She teaches creative writing at The New School University in New York.

Eliot Weinberger is the author of seventeen books, including *Nineteen Ways of Looking at Wang Wei, Outside Stories, What I Heard about Iraq, Karmic Traces, An Elemental Thing, The Stars,* and *Works on Paper.* The recipient of the PEN/Kolovakos Award, the Order of the Aztec Eagle from the Mexican government, and the National Book Critics Circle Award, Weinberger has also translated 20 books by writers such as Bei Dao, Jorge Louis Borges, and Octavio Paz, for whom Weinberger translated ten books alone.

Shawn Wen is a multimedia artist whose radio has aired on *This American Life, Studio 360,* and *Freakonomics,* among other programs. Her video work has screened at the Museum of Modern Art in New York, the Carpenter Center for Visual Art at Harvard University, and the Camden International Film Festival, and her installations have exhibited the Via di Sant'Anna Gallery in Rome, among other places. The recipient of Royce Fellowship

and the Third Coast Scholarship, Wen is a producer on the radio program *The State of Things.*

Joe Wenderoth is the author of *Letters to Wendy's*, *If I Don't Breathe How Do I Sleep*, *No Real Light*, *It Is If I Speak*, *Disfortune*, and *The Holy Spirit of Life: Essays Written for John Ashcroft's Secret Self.* In 2003, the One Yellow Rabbit theater company produced an adaptation of his highly popular *Letters to Wendy's*, featuring Bruce McCulloch of *The Kids in the Hall.* The recipient of numerous literary awards, Wenderoth teaches creative writing at the University of California at Davis.

Paul West is the author of 50 books of fiction, poetry, and nonfiction, including the classics *The Very Rich Hours of Count von Stauffenberg*, *Words for a Deaf Daughter*, *Sporting with Amaryllis*, *A Stroke of Genius: Illness and Self-Discovery*, *The Shadow Factory*, and *The Dry Danube: A Hitler Forgery*, which first began with his essay of the same name in *Seneca Review.* The recipient of a multitude of awards, including the Chevalier of the Order of Arts and Letters from France, West lives in Ithaca, NY.